WHAT OF THE NIGHT?

Personal essays

by

Stephen Carter

Provo, Utah

Earlier versions of these essays appeared as follows:

"Writing as Repentance" originally published in *Sunstone*, issue 154.

"Act II" originally published as "Wherein I Justify My Existence," in *Sunstone*, issue 151.

"The Weight of Priesthood" originally published in *Dialogue: A Journal of Mormon Thought*, Vol. 38 No. 3.

"Smoke and Mirrors" originally published in *Sunstone*, issue 142.

"Winter Light" originally published in *Sunstone*, issue 139.

"The Departed" originally published in *Sunstone*, issue 146.

"A Brief Tour of England: My Year With Gene" originally published in *Dialogue: A Journal of Mormon Thought*, vol. 35, no. 1.

"The Calling" originally published in *Sunstone*, issue 148.

"A Parable of Fish" originally published in *The Black Ridge Review*, issue 2.

"Last Supper" originally published in *Dialogue: A Journal of Mormon Thought*, vol. 35, no. 2.

© 2010 by Stephen Carter

ISBN 978-0-9843603-1-4

Cover illustration and illustration on page 166 by Anna Waschke.

All rights reserved.
Printed in the U.S.A.

Published by Zarahemla Books
869 East 2680 North
Provo, UT 84604
info@zarahemlabooks.com
ZarahemlaBooks.com

For my wife,
who kept listening

Contents

A Parable of Fish 1

A Brief Tour of England:
My Year with Gene 11

Act II 26

The Weight of Priesthood 33

Smoke and Mirrors 63

On the Virtues of Easy Listening 83

Last Supper 91

Winter Light 97

The Departed 115

Isaiah Chapter Six 131

The Calling 139

Writing as Repentance 159

A Parable of Fish

A RUBBERY YANK. A figure eight of surprise. It wasn't pondweed this time.

All the way to the Canyon View pond, a little spot of giddy hope had been jelling in my stomach. It jumped up to my chest whenever I remembered, again, that I was on my way to fish for the first time in my life. Visions of this noble sport filled my mind: the easy posture of the fisherman silhouetted against a sunset, the adrenalin of the catch, the strategic battle to cajole the fish toward the shore and finally, in a grand flourish of pole and fish, to land it. And, of course, the snapshot of the warrior, triumphant.

Just before we hit the pond, my Cub Scout pack gathered around in a little blue circle and prayed. Sister Williams, our den mother, asked God to keep us safe and help us catch some fish. And now here it was, the consummation of my hopes and Sister Williams's prayer tugging on my line. It was indeed a grand moment. I saw the fish, a bitty rainbow trout, looking at me from the water with its expressionless eyes and a round, open mouth. The first catch of the day.

I actually caught two that day, and they both went into one of the plastic bread bags Sister Williams had brought along. The bag leapt and wormed on the grass. Possessed Wonder Bread.

The afternoon turned out to be quite successful for everyone. Sister Williams beamed at her little scouts, admiring their fish prodigiously with her wide first-grade-teacher eyes. Best of all, no hooks had been threaded through human lips or embedded in eyeballs. Our prayers had been answered.

I could feel the delicate weight of my two tiny fish as Sister Williams drove us home. Their placid curves bowed the bottom of the bag. I was about to enter a world painted by Norman Rockwell: the conquering fisher striding through the door, brandishing his catch to the drop-mouthed wonder of younger siblings and pipe-chomping satisfaction of the father (of course, my father would have to make do with suspender thumbing or something because Mormons don't smoke). It was a wonderful, simple, all-American story.

I marched proudly through the kitchen door, my fish swinging none too inconspicuously in front of me. But the room was empty. Except for my mother who was opening a can of tuna. She eyed the swinging bag in my hand like it was an alligator and grabbed at the telephone. She tapped out a familiar electronic melody. The Neils. Yes, apparently they knew how to clean a fish. She ushered me out the door into the evening.

I lived on a simple, rectangular suburban block, inside a house that had the same floor plan as all the others. Most of my neighbors were Mormons of one kind or another. The only exception to this rule was the Neils, the Catholics who lived on the other side of the block. I liked the Neils. The oldest boy, Steven, was one of my best friends. He was a short, round kid with sharp eyes and fast legs.

It seemed strange, however, that my mom was voluntarily sending me over to Steven's house. He could out-swear a sailor, having been scrupulously trained by his trucker father, who, along with his wife, smoked and drank like no one I had ever known. Of course, I had never known anyone who smoked or drank before then. The only other person comparable was my grandmother, who drank Diet Pepsi. And added to all that, the first dirty story I ever heard was from Steven, though it turned out kind of anticlimactic for me, as I lacked the vocabulary for a proper appreciation. Pretty much everything that happened over at Steven's house was disapproved of by my church and by my mother.

I sometimes wondered what the Neils' eternal status would be. Which kingdom would they land in, once their lives were over? As much as I liked them, I was pretty sure they were the lost people in the painting of Lehi's dream—an image I had often seen during my Sunday school classes. The painting showed a dark landscape filled with a sticky mist that reminded me of the clouds that billowed over the local steel refinery. Some filthy rivers slithered around, sucking down tiny frantic bodies. And in the far right of the picture a giant canyon waited for blinded people to walk off its edge. Wandering through all this were the lost souls, twisted and dark like firecrackered army figures. I knew that they were the ones who were "dwindling in unbelief."

Dwindling seemed like a good word to describe these people, toddling in circles, bumping against things in the dark. But through the center of the picture there was a rod of iron, set up like a partition at Disneyland rides, and a few people were holding onto it so tight you'd think they were in a tug of war. The rod led through the mists and the swamps, but eventually it wound up at the foot of a white tree that seemed to have hundred-watt light bulbs for fruit. The Tree of Life.

The picture was comforting to me, as I was certainly one who clung to the iron rod. The way to the celestial kingdom was strait and narrow. There was no mistaking it. It was like the streets of my rectangular suburb with signs for every road.

But there was one spot in the picture where the rod of iron, and the people who clutched it, disappeared altogether. Consumed, finally, by the mists and deepest quagmires. I often wondered, what in the world is happening in there?

   The sun had set when I arrived at Steven's house. It was the only one on the block painted a dark brown. The rest of the houses were white, or pale blue, or yellow (like my house). His house was also the only one with a chain-link fence that kept a huge black husky dog in the yard, barking heartfelt curses at passersby and daring someone to just try and open the gate. Fortunately, he knew me, so I got in with only a rabid glare and a chainsaw growl that vibrated all windowpanes within a twenty-foot radius. The gate clinked shut behind me. I knocked on the door.
   Steven's mother opened the door, and tobacco smoke crept out. It had rooted itself in the carpet and furniture, a veil as thick as quilt batting. I could see an open can of Budweiser inside on the kitchen table.
   Steven's mother was completely different from my fresh, dimply den mother. She had an obscure shade of thin brown hair. Her

face was dark and wrinkled, as if she fed a blast furnace twelve hours a day. Her voice was dry and serrated as a rusty saw blade. My whole image of her could be wrapped up in the way she would answer the phone, "Yyyyellow," with the Y drawn out for a few beats. But this yellow was the color of old leaves or teeth, not the bright pastel of my den mother's blouse. She was a leaf of a woman, but out of all that thinness, she could utter mighty words that still reverberate in my mind the way a prophecy might. One day I was in the kitchen with her when she found out that the Cub Scout cake contest was that night. "Great God Almighty!" she thundered, her voice like an avalanche of bones. I figure that God heard her utterance, blasphemous or not, because that night Steven showed up with a cake shaped and decorated like his father's diesel truck. It won second prize, coming in close behind the X-wing fighter.

Just like the outside of the house, the inside was dark. A film of tar had aged the white walls, and light seemed reluctant to spread itself around too much. It mostly remained in pools beneath the lamps and low-hanging lights. In the middle of the dark living-room wall hung a large cross. It spread itself over about a third of the wall. On it was the bony body of a dying Jesus, his hands curled over the nails, his loincloth limping toward one thigh, head lolling.

    I recognized this Jesus only because I remembered seeing a picture of the crucifixion a few times in church. But it wasn't like this thing stuck to the Neils' wall. The pictures I was used to were like scenes from a trade show: three demonstration crucifees on display and a few gawkers below being watched by the lazy eye of a Roman guard. Everyone was too small to have details. I couldn't identify any pain in those pictures. Even the three dying men seemed to have just nodded off in a pleasant doze on their crosses. Well, that whole scene wasn't the important part anyway. The important thing was that Jesus arose three days later and is still living—even today. According to the pictures I had seen to illustrate this fact, he had also been shampooed, laundered, and blow-dried for the resurrection. Was this wretch on the Neils' wall the god of my religion?

If this did happen to be the same Jesus, I wondered why he was hanging so painfully inside a house whose owners measured their beer in cases and talked up casual monsoons of obscenities that would have earned me a year's worth of mouth washings. Why was this Jesus even more naked than the sleek woman on the poster in their basement?

Steven's dad lumbered into the light from the dark hallway. He had Popeye forearms with the requisite tattoos, and a bulging rectangle in his breast pocket.

My stomach did its little jump again as I watched Steven's dad's chunky hands pick up the small, helpless body of my fish. It shone like a newly minted silver dollar. Glass, or a soap bubble; steel, perhaps. The fish that came in answer to my den mother's prayer.

"First you stick your knife up here," Steven's dad said. He slid the blade into a small hole on the bottom of the fish and tore the narrow belly upward to its chin.

"That's its butthole, isn't it, Dad?" Steven asked.

"Yes, son, it is."

I watched, horrified and enamored with the naming and destruction of the parts. The little heart went pop like a grape between Steven's dad's thick fingers. The digestive tract, like a rubber skeleton, was flung on the counter. The pointed head was flipped backwards, as if it were the top of a Zippo lighter. The jelly along the fish's spine ran down his thumb.

Before I knew it, I had two limp, slimy fish splayed on the counter, eyes staring toward the ceiling. I could open their bodies like a book. I felt a little sick. Steven's mom gave me a fresh plastic bag to carry my cleansed fish in, and I walked out the door passing the Son of God pegged on a hunk of wood to die.

As I walked back around the darkened block that night, I started wishing that my bag were opaque. I no longer wanted to see my fishes' bodies. They were dimming quickly—a jot and tittle passing away. No longer perfect bullets. Stark, ragged flesh with a thick smell about them.

A Brief Tour of England: My Year with Gene

WE IN UTAH VALLEY State College's Center for the Study of Ethics were sardines, but we were happy sardines. Our office (formerly a mythical beast called a "faculty lounge") housed the chair of the humanities department, the director of the ethics center, Melanie (the ultra-competent secretarial glue that held the office together), and me (a research assistant). We didn't mind being crammed together in the little room, considering ourselves lucky to have anything that resembled an office in space-tight UVSC, where all unoccupied nooks were metamorphosing into offices. Not even bathrooms were safe. Fifty feet down the hall, in a converted broom closet, stood the outer satellite of the center: Eugene England's office.

Though Gene didn't spend much time

in the ethics center itself, his presence still permeated our office. The closet burst with the lawn signs he had made by the dozens to advertise the conferences he sponsored on campus, and my ever-ringing phone provided a constant background noise to the office activity. Nine times out of ten, it was Gene on the other end.

When people familiar with his projects, articles, and books discovered I worked for Gene, then writer-in-residence at UVSC, most of them assumed I must spend my days talking theology with him or researching his next essay. It is true that I talked with him a lot—maybe once every three minutes. Gene's mind, I found, works on the fly. He called to talk about anything that came into his mind—the moment it came into his mind. I could hear Melanie giggling sometimes when my phone rang for the thirtieth time that day.

"Steve? Gene here. I want you to get fifty more copies of the conference flyer and put them in my box. Oh, and I want to change the lawn signs this time to include the time and place for the keynote speaker. Do you think you can get Gustav to do that?"

Five seconds later the phone rang again. Gene had remembered that he also wanted engraved invitations for the local dignitaries, a copy of the article on the Bear River massacre that may have been published in October by the *Salt Lake Tribune*, and addresses for three people who had just moved.

By the time I had opened the word processor to print out the flyer, Gene was on the phone trying to remember if the conference participants had been paid and if, by any chance, I had found that *Tribune* article yet.

Eventually I started treating myself to a liberal use of the voice-mail system when Gene's assignments piled too high. However, I could buy only limited time with that strategy. Failing to get me on the phone, Gene would come find me. He knew my tactics.

None of the foregoing should be construed to mean that I didn't love working for Gene. Everyone who has had personal contact with him can attest that his tremendous tolerance and genuine charity made up for all his eccentricities. Gene is the only boss I ever had who hugged me almost daily.

• • •

During my first six months with Gene, he kept me busy with the kind of work only he could produce: the impossible kind.

He would dash into the office an hour before the last mail pickup and earnestly inform me that he wanted his list of three-hundred friends and colleagues to receive one more invitation to his latest conference. I would start the work with the blunted enthusiasm I would use to humor the whims of an insane man. But Gene's tidal wave of faith, which he could produce spontaneously in concert with his latest project, had already caught me up to its crest, though I didn't know it.

Carried by this invisible tsunami, we somehow completed Gene's Herculean projects nine times out of ten. We printed address labels, made copies, and folded and stuffed envelopes faster than Vaughn J. Featherstone can spit out a talk. Then Gene would run outside just before I had licked the last ten envelope flaps and drive his Toyota 4Runner up to the door, poised to snatch the batch of still-moist envelopes from me. He sometimes left a little rubber on the pavement as he sped off to the campus mailroom, where all the elements combined to pull off yet another miracle for the man.

After these ordeals, I would often slump, temporarily exhausted, into my chair, small paper cuts on my fingertips, envelope glue still coating my tongue, and say to myself, "O ye of little faith." I wondered if Gene had some genealogical connections with the Biblical Joshua, inheriting a small bit of the ability to stop time when something really needed to get done.

We pulled off other huge stunts, too, like the time historian Jan Shipps came to UVSC. The Regan Theater, which had been completely booked for the next year, just happened to have as its only free night the very evening Jan came: Valentine's Day. I snagged the theater only one day before her arrival.

Though a good 99.9 percent of Gene's frenetic projects actually worked out, he still worried like no one I have ever known. Sometimes at 10:00 p.m. the night before a conference, a harried Gene would call me at my home confessing, "I can't sleep, Steve. I don't know if anyone is going to come tomorrow. So pray for us, all right?" Gene was my hugging and praying boss.

Perhaps to assuage his hyperactive worry gland, Gene advertised prolifically. His lists of friends and contacts were voluminous, and every one of them usually received at least two separate invitations to Gene's to-dos, as well as extra copies with a small note asking them to hand them around to their friends. We badgered local reporters, plastered posters all over the UVSC and BYU campuses, and filled the e-mail inboxes of anyone even remotely interested in Mormon studies. None could escape.

In 2000 Gene received a rare $25,000 grant from the National Endowment for the Humanities to start a Mormon cultural studies program on the UVSC campus. Though I was swamped with a new volley of Gene's rapid-fire calls and all the assignments they brought, I realize now that those were happy days. We were busy, but Gene, with his boundless energy, pulled it all off, putting together conference after conference, seminar after seminar, and generally turning the campus on its ear.

In the midst of it all, Gene became terribly sick for three days. Once, when I had to call for instructions, I could barely hear his voice on the other end of the line.

"I don't know what's happening to me, Steve," he said. "I've never been this sick in my life." He dropped the phone and didn't pick it back up.

A few days later he seemed to be back on his feet. But his face, which had once been too full of life to give any credence to its age lines, had withered discernibly. His grand eyebrows, the kind reserved for wizards, started to droop lower over his half-moon eyes. He no longer sat in chairs; he folded into them like a marionette. A sleeping pad and a pillow appeared in his office, and he would frequently call me to ask that I wake him in time for appointments. Sometimes I had to knock two or three times before I could hear any movement in the room.

One day Gene took me into his office and started to talk. "I don't know what's wrong with me, Steve. I'm just so tired all the time, and I get so depressed. Nothing like this has ever happened to me before."

He said that sentence often, almost like a mantra, "Nothing like this has ever happened to me before." His health, which had apparently accompanied him throughout his life even more faithfully than taxes, had been pulled out from under him like a tablecloth in a Flamenco dance.

He groped for some reason to explain this black hole inside him. He hypothesized at length with me a few times. At first he thought it might be a kind of post-traumatic stress disorder resulting from his last experiences at BYU, where some of his writings had incurred displeasure from the BYU and LDS Church hierarchy. "You don't know what it was like to hear what I heard from men I believe have authority from God," he said.

Gene seemed to envision some sort of mental cancer inflicted during those hard days, corroding him silently from within while his body and life had continued, unsuspecting. He started sending me out to the library to find books on post-traumatic stress disorder and depression.

Sometimes at night when everyone had gone home, either Melanie or I would be startled by the muted hum of the office printer spitting out sheets of paper. It always took a few seconds for me to remember that Gene had a connection to the printer as well and he was the one behind these mystery printouts. He often forgot to retrieve his papers, so Melanie or I would take them out of the printer tray and set them in his box. Most of the pages had poetry printed on them. I realized later that they were pieces Gene had turned out during his free time in his office. I caught the basic drift of the poems by glancing at the pages. One still haunts me.

It starts by describing the trek of a woman and her three children through Central America. They are trying to escape an oppressive husband and government by taking a one-way hike to another country. While crossing the railroad tracks, one of the children is struck and killed by a train. Then the poem switches to an incident where a president of the LDS Church is warned by the Spirit to return to his seat on the train. He obeys just before the train hits a bump that would have thrown him from his previous position standing on the small patio at the rear of the train, probably to his death.

The poem ends with Gene talking with Jesus Christ. Gene's character demands to know which of these situations God had his hand in. The Savior turns to him, tears streaming down his face, and with "his brow set like flint" replies, "Both."

Despites his illness, Gene continued to plan seminars for the next semester and for his study-abroad trip to London. But he also continued to deteriorate. During the seminars and lectures he attended, his characteristic pose—legs and arms crossed, head cocked slightly, denoting deep thought and attention—sagged into sporadic bouts of slumber, his head bobbing as if it were floating gently on slow wavelets of water.

Gene had one final upswing, and we all fell quickly and optimistically into the habit of believing that the old (meaning young) Gene was back with us again. We breathed this small pocket of clean air deeply just before the storm hit.

Early on a pleasant February morning, Charlotte dragged Gene to the hospital for an emergency surgery that left him looking, as Robert Kirby put it, "as if he had been given a good work over with a highly effective tire iron." The reports sounded grim: a lobe incised, cysts removed, and no promises that the cancer inside his brain had been completely removed.

Imagine my surprise the next morning when my phone rang and Gene started issuing instructions through the half of his mouth that still worked. Charlotte kept trying to take the phone away from him, but Gene had awakened remembering that the plays and flats needed reserving for the study-abroad program. Nothing could stop him, not even brain surgery. We were all glad he seemed to have retained his personality and thinking power despite having fewer gray cells to work with.

What he didn't have, however, was the use of the left side of his body. With his almost embarrassing candor, Gene told me on the phone about two weeks after his operation that he was doing all right except for the fact that he could not yet "eliminate" by himself. Charlotte almost got the phone away from him that time.

"It's discouraging to see how much I have to do to recover," he told me, "but I have lots of help and love." His goal was to rehabilitate in time to go to London that summer.

After the surgery, Gene's previous depressions began to make sense. We started to understand that the pressure leveled on his brain from the growing cysts was the most likely cause. Instead of suffering only from psychological distress, the inner space of Gene's own body had started to boil with cancer. The question we had was: How far had the cancer spread? The doctors couldn't tell.

One day, I went to meet a few of Gene's colleagues at the Utah Valley Regional Medical Center and visit him. As I waited for them, I caught sight of Gene's head, recognizable by the huge hieroglyph of a scar the surgeons had carved into his skull. Gray stubble had just started to grow back. Charlotte was wheeling Gene down the hall toward the therapy pool. He saw me, too, and raised his good right hand, flashing one of his famous smiles at me.

In the therapy room, we watched as Gene limped painstakingly through the simple exercises his therapist had assigned. One side of his body still retained the toned muscle he had maintained through his years of daily jogs, but the muscles and skin on the other half of his body hung from his bones like thick honey. Gene worked methodically in the therapy pool to reconnect the left side of his body to his brain. His focus on these rudimentary tasks reminded me of the intellectual intensity of his best essays.

Half an hour later we sat in Gene's hospital room. Dressed in a T-shirt and sweat pants, his left arm posed, mannequin-like, on a tray extending from his wheelchair, Gene talked with us about literature, theology, and one of his most recent ideas: writing an article about tidbits of information Christ gives about his own mortal life in the Doctrine and Covenants. But soon he tired. In the course of our good-byes he told us, "Some people don't believe me when I say this, but I have spent my entire life being an apologist for the gospel, because I know it's true."

I saw Gene only once after that. He flagged

me down in the parking lot outside the David O. McKay Events Center, just after the Dalai Lama had spoken. He gave me an avalanche of instructions, as if he had never missed a day at UVSC.

"Check my phone messages," he said, "and my e-mail. And see if you can find my file on Scott Card's *Pastwatch*. It should be in my"—his eyebrows buckled in concentration—"right-hand bottom desk drawer. And if it's not there, it may be on the floor next to the bookcase—unless, of course, I put it in the filing cabinet. Oh, and Steve, make sure to remind the study-abroad students of the next orientation meeting. Make sure we have cookies and punch there."

A few weeks later, I received my last Gene-related assignment. "Gently and carefully," I was told, "clean out Gene's office." The thought shocked me, even though we had received news that cancer had been found in Gene's spine, leaving us almost without hope.

Fortunately Gene had been occupying this particular office for less than a year, because already his ineffable filing system covered most of his office floor while the filing cabinets remained mostly empty, except for a Tupperware container full of trail mix and a few other odds and ends.

Anyone who knows Gene could predict my findings as I sorted through his stacks and loaded boxes. Scores of books of Mormon literature and Shakespeare filled the shelves, along with a stockpile of Gene's own published books and photographs and playbills. One of Mark England's mammoth pencil drawings towered over the desk, telling Gene's biography in a geologic language of amoebic continents, states, and towns baled together by whorls of telephone wires. On the back wall, portraits of Dickenson, Keats, and Melville watched over my shoulder as I scoured Gene's desk, clearing out little jars of almond butter, vitamins, and unused sticky notes. Finally, I packed his four-in-one scripture set. Compact, brown, and well used, the book had Gene's name on it, literally and figuratively. Though his desk was an ever-changing landscape of papers and books, it was always this book that managed to remain on top of it all.

Act II

This inaugural editorial appeared in the October 2008 issue of Sunstone *magazine.*

IT'S KIND OF SCARY TO SEE my name sidle into its place on *Sunstone*'s masthead next to the worthy names of Dan Wotherspoon, Elbert Eugene Peck, Peggy Fletcher Stack, Allen Roberts, and Scott Kenney. I feel like an Osric suddenly called upon to play Hamlet.

Whether there was a divinity that shaped this particular fate of mine, you'll have to judge for yourself. Let me tell you how I got here.

My story starts in 1997 when I first met Eugene England. He had just become writer-in-residence at Utah Valley State College (now Utah Valley University) and was in the initial stages of planning what is now the

Mormon studies program. By a great stroke of luck, he hired me as his administrative assistant, and I became deeply involved in his work. I got to sit in on both private and public scholarly symposia with some of the most interesting people in Mormon studies, such as Armand Mauss, Carol Cornwall Madsen, Jan Shipps, Terryl Givens, and the late Dean May. This period was a formative one for me, because for the first time in my life, I heard Mormonism discussed with discipline, intelligence, and spirit.

I realized only later how unique my tenure with Gene was. Few undergraduates are privileged to take part in gatherings in which religious and scholarly discourse is carried on with such skill and wisdom. I attribute the unique spirit of these meetings to Gene's commitment to Joseph Smith's concept of "proving contraries." When one proves contraries, Gene always argued, you aren't doing so to identify which is right and which is wrong but to experience the tension between them. It is the experience of dwelling in this tension that makes you wiser.

The scholars Gene brought together were skilled in the art of dwelling in tension. They didn't jump ship when the conversation got hard. They didn't bail when someone challenged their ideas. In fact, they saw these moments as opportunities. They knew that ideas can grow only when they are interacting. And the best way to make ideas interact is to put them in tension.

A few days after Gene died, I moved to Alaska and began a master of fine arts program in creative writing. Then, just because I could, I also finished a Ph.D. in narrative studies.

During that time, I became fascinated with the structure of stories. I discovered that the great characters of fiction are those who are stretched between two competing values. Think of Chaim Potok's Asher Lev, stretched between his devotion to his religion and his passion for art. Think of *The Merchant of Venice*, where justice and mercy vie for the souls of Shylock and Portia.

I also learned that the great stories of the world have second acts. This may seem like a silly thing to say, but so many stories set up the problem (the job of the first act) and then resolve it (the job of the third act) with little to no struggle in between. I'm here to tell you that it's the struggle that makes a story great, because that's the time when the opposing forces are at their most powerful, when they wreak their full havoc on the character. Rest assured that any character emerging from the second act without scars is a cheater.

I began to see that Gene was right. Those who dwell in the tension, those who are willing to go through their second act, gain much. Those who jump out too early lose much. Perhaps this is the wisdom behind the adage, "Endure to the end."

That is how the foundation for my passion and commitment to the mission of Sunstone was laid. Sunstone is the place where Mormons can come to dwell in the tensions that arise from their religion and from the rest of the world. It happens to all us. We find ourselves inexplicably pummeled by the slings and arrows of outrageous fortune. During these times, we need a place to wrestle in spirit, as Jacob did, as Job did, as Jesus did. It needs to be an independent place; it needs to be open, respectful, and rigorous.

Thus, Sunstone is necessarily a place of labor. No spiritual journey is a primrose path; it is a "steep and thorny way to heaven," as Hamlet put it. The people you find at Sunstone are not the ones who have jumped. They are the ones who are still trying to navigate their vessels between the whirlpool of Charybdis and the teeth of Scylla. They are the ones who have been brave enough to plunge deep into the second act of their story.

But getting through the second act isn't the end.

As Elie Wiesel said, "I believe that whatever we receive, we must share. When [I] endure an experience, the experience cannot stay with me alone. It must be opened, it must become an offering; it must be deepened and given and shared."[1] The act of composing your story is a heroic journey in itself. "It is essential that the writer undergo the journey," playwright David Mamet says. "That's why writing never gets any easier."[2]

And then we, the audience, become the beneficiary of that double journey. "The true drama . . . calls for the hero to exercise will," Mamet continues, "to create in front of us, on the stage, his or her own character, the strength to continue. It is her striving to understand, to correctly assess, to face her own character [. . .] that inspires us—and gives the drama power to cleanse and enrich our own character."[3]

My editorial philosophy for Sunstone will follow in Gene's tradition. There are contraries all around us, and we will prove them. We will wrestle within their tensions. We will do so with rigor and artistry. We will open the conversation. We will plunge into our second acts. And when we find our way out the other side, we will shape our journey into a story and share it.

As the novelist E. M. Forester writes, "One can, at all events, show one's own little light here, one's own poor little trembling flame, with the knowledge that it is not the only light that is shining in the darkness, and not the only one which the darkness does not comprehend."[4]

NOTES

1. Elie Wiesel, "God Is God Because He Remem-

bers," *All Things Considered*, 7 April 2008, http://www.thisibelieve.org (accessed September 16, 2008).
2. David Mamet, *Three Uses of the Knife: On the Nature and Purpose of Drama* (New York: Vintage Books, 2000), 19.
3. Ibid., 43.
4. E. M. Forster, *Two Cheers for Democracy* (New York: Harcourt Trade Publishers, 1962), 76.

The Weight of Priesthood

Winner of the Dialogue Young Writer Award, and cited as notable writing in The Best American Spiritual Writing 2006.

I WAS EIGHT YEARS OLD one March Sunday. The chapel curtains were bright with the springtime sun, as if angels were standing outside. The church itself was new, built only a year or two earlier out in the middle of some farmland. Cows were the closest neighbors. The brown bricks and stoic wood paneling gave the building a solid feel—unlike my stomach, which was clutching and jerking. One of my buddies, David, was sitting on a chair at the front of the chapel, and large, suit-coated men had gathered around him. I was next in line.

My whole extended family had come to see me. After all, I was one of the first grandchildren to go through a confirmation. Later we'd all get together at our house and eat sandwiches, but first, I had to take the hot seat. I was a little frightened. But it was a fear that had never entered my heart before. I knew the metallic pang from the anticipation of a parent's wrath. I understood the snatch of panic when older kids came after me. But this was the first time I had the fear of God in me.

Is that what you call it? Fear? I can't call it respect or awe; those seem passive nouns. I need something active to describe the feeling of coming up against the major powers I had heard about all my life. Fear is when you are going to do something, and you don't know exactly what will happen as a consequence. It's when you wonder if you are in over your head. When you wonder if you might lose something. Or be crushed by what you are given.

Weight. Yeah, there was a lot of weight to this whole process. It had started the day before that fateful Sunday, when I stuck my toe into the baptismal font water, warm as amniotic fluid. I felt the pull of the water as I walked down the stairs. The legs of my white jumpsuit flowered out, and air blew out of my collar as the water gained ground. By the time I had hit the bottom step, I was in almost up to my chest. It was a little hard to breathe. I had to hold my arms up to keep them clear of the water. My dad took my hands in the way we had practiced. I looked up at the mirror that hung over the water. It was there to help the people in the back see what was going on. It gave them a bird's eye view. Kind of like how God was seeing me, I guess.

Dad held his arm to the square and said a short prayer. It told me that I was being baptized by someone who had authority from God. Then I went down. The idea, I was told, was to bend your knees and lean back. Kind of like doing the limbo. That way none of your hair would stick up, or your belly. You had to be totally immersed; otherwise you had to do it again. And as even an eight-year-old knew, a second time is anticlimactic. Under the water I heard the gabble of bubbles and a rushing sound. I felt completely alone. Then I thought, *I won-*

der when I'll come up again? and the world exploded around me. I was back with water in my eyes and my jumpsuit clinging to my body. I couldn't see much at all. Not even all the little kids that had scooted to the font so they could see better. I stumbled out of the font. Pure.

    Well. That was it, I guessed. I was clean. No sins clung to me. It was a pleasant feeling for a second or two, until I started shivering in my wet clothes. My dad led me into the changing room where David and his dad were . . . well, changing. I had not anticipated this situation. The last time I had been anywhere close to naked in the church was two months before when I had made my trial attempt at using the standing urinal, not realizing that one did not have to pull down one's pants in order to use it, though the people waiting in line may have understood that principle. But that was behind me now. I was clean. Except for the fact that I had to take off my jumpsuit and change into clean underwear in front of three other people. I shot a furtive glance at David. Still suited and shivering like me, he was watching me out of the corner of his eye. I looked at my dad, hoping for a precedent to follow. I had never seen so much hair in such unexpected places. Perhaps I could study the tiles and make conversation until everyone was done changing—except that Dad was patting me on the back and telling me to get moving.

David and I locked eyes—just daring each other to look. I unzipped mine. He unzipped his. As long as I watched him, I was sure he wouldn't do anything funny. One arm. Steady. Down the torso. Hips. Oh my gosh. Underwear doesn't come on easily when you're sopping wet. But we made do.

Dang. Did this mean I had already committed a sin? It was kind of hard to tell. David better just keep his mouth shut.

But here I was, Sunday, sitting on a hard chair at the front of the chapel in the center of the circle of men. I was staring at their belt buckles and smelling their Old Spice. They went into blessing stance: left hand on one another's backs, right hand on my head. The weight of the priesthood was upon me. My dad started praying, telling me to receive the Holy Ghost. I waited. Nothing palpable—except the weight. There must have been ten right hands on my head, all charged with the priesthood of God, and a few pounds each. He said more, but I didn't quite catch it all. Then the prayer ended and the second ordinance, unessential but traditional, started: the shaking of hands. Why did we feel compelled to do this? Well, all Mormons do it after a blessing. Kind of a thank-you gesture. The blessing just doesn't feel finished otherwise. Perhaps it's another contact, in case the head wasn't clean enough. One more circuit for the Spirit of God to enter through.

    I bore my testimony that day. I don't remember what I said, but the weight of the priesthood stayed with me. Mostly in my neck. That was the thing I remembered. To receive God is to receive weight. It had been in my wet clothes and in the hands of the priesthood bearers. And then, ten years later, in my bones.

    I was an elder. They announced me in stake conference. I stood so everyone could see me. I had a new white shirt and tie for the occasion. The whole extended family was there, because I was the first. We gathered in our living room a few hours later. I sat in a chair, and the men moved in around me, forming a circle and placing left hands on backs, right hands on my head. Now I looked at their chests. But the weight was exactly the same, though my neck held up better.

This time it wasn't the Spirit of God I was receiving, but His priesthood. An eighteen-year-old with God's power? It seemed as likely that He would give an eight-year-old His spirit. But that's what they had told me for years. Those men, so ponderous and steady, had latent power rippling under their skin. The kind of power that could heal the sick, comfort the downtrodden, and call down the might of heaven. As the prayer began, the fear entered me again. An active fear of a God who was acting upon me.

Their hands lifted from my head, and I was returned to my normal gravity. I stood to complete the circuit. And felt something. The marrow in my bones seemed heavier, solid. Normally a skinny, geeky kid, I suddenly felt like there was a live wire strung through my joints. I sat down and put my arms around my girlfriend. And for the first time, I felt like I could actually protect her. Like I was a real man. A priesthood bearer.

    Except it took a while to turn on the juice. This happens to me a lot. I get all psyched—spirit in my britches—and then the laundry needs doing for the next six months. The boil slows to a simmer. For a long time after my ordination there weren't any dead who needed raising. The sick, having heard of my new powers, had not shown themselves at my door. The gravity melted slowly, or else my muscles adapted. Whichever. But I knew there was a catch to getting the priesthood. The church just doesn't go around ordaining eighteen-year-olds to be elders for nothing. You have to sign your name to something else first: mission papers. In order to be a real man, you've got to head out into the world for two years under the church's flag. You have to join that army of boys with black nametags and ties. And when you go out into the world to preach the gospel, you really should have some idea of how to use the priesthood.

    At least, I thought so. There are two great story settings in the Mormon church, the pioneer trek and the mission field. In both of these dramatic settings, a person is not surprised to hear about miracles. They are those uncharted countries where ordinary life is exploded. Where there be dragons and cherubim. What Mormon has not heard of the packs of demons attacking Heber C. Kimball and his companions as they proselytized in England? How the hooked shapes leapt at them, and how the elders fought them off with their own fists and the priesthood. Who has not heard of a child being brought back from death's door by the ministrations of two twenty-year-old missionaries? But it is one thing to hear those stories from the mouths of missionaries returning home from the mission field or from teachers in Sunday school. It is another to actually enter them. God has to fill your bones.

I wanted to rev the divine engine, prime the priesthood pump. Get that power moving. I figured, since God gave it to me, maybe He'd also give me a chance to use it. So I asked Him about it for a few weeks. It was a half-hearted request because, frankly, the thought of administering to someone scared me to death. Large, Old-Spiced men with heavy hands gave blessings. I was as close to Atlas Bodybuilding's derided ninety-eight-pound weakling as one could be, and I wore Speed Stick. Certainly I didn't qualify. But the fact was, I had the priesthood.

One evening, a few weeks before I left for my mission, I was sitting in the chapel of the Manti temple. This temple is located in a tiny town in the middle of miles of Utah's sagebrush and sun. The original settlers thought their little burg would grow quickly, so they built a temple—the second to be dedicated in Utah—on the hill east of town. It's an odd building, a kind of mutated Puritan-style church house, or diminutive castle, with towers on each end of the building. But instead of being steepled, they are topped by a trapezoidal taper. The whole building is made of limestone, solid as the mountain it's built upon. During the day its silhouette is visible for miles. At night it lights up, stunning the whole valley. It's my favorite temple. I'm not sure there are any Mormons from Utah who don't have a pioneer-built temple as their favorite. There's an element of sweat and studiousness that draws us to them. Men and women sacrificed to build those early structures. Some of them are our own flesh and blood. A million stories surround each one of them. And you can feel it. Like priesthood.

I was dressed in my white clothing, waiting for the next endowment session to start. I was looking forward to the ritual. In the Manti temple it is especially dramatic, as the walls and ceilings of the large rooms are painted with scenes from the creation, the Garden of Eden, the telestial world, the terrestial world, and finally God's kingdom. As you move from room to room the light increases, giving you the feeling that you're getting closer to God with each step.

But that was the night the lights went out in Manti. A storm had chased us there, and apparently it had struck something important. My mom, dad, and aunt were sitting with me when the room went black. As the little emergency lights came up, one of the temple patrons walked in and told us we'd have to wait till the electricity came back before we could start our session. My dad and aunt walked the halls to console my dad's bum back. A car accident early in his twenties had doomed him to a life of back pain and periodic migraine headaches. I moved to the back of the chapel to get away from the tapestry at the front. It's an attempt at a Raphaelesque group with women and children. And it's awful—the people's noses are huge, and the babies' heads are deformed. But the pioneers did it. So we keep it. After all, they did a great job on the building itself.

I talked to God in the dark of His temple. I gave him the lowdown again: I'm headed out and I don't want to be a total greenhorn, OK? Just give me something to break me in. I'll take anything.

The lights came back on. The air conditioning started pushing the air again. I walked up and sat next to my mom. She leaned over and said, "You know, your dad's back and headaches have been hurting him a lot lately. I bet he'd appreciate a blessing from you."

Well, there you go.

I wasn't familiar at the time with the biblical parable of the sleeping housemaster. If I had been, I might have looked on this incident a little differently. Jesus said that prayer is sometimes like a fellow going to a man's house to ask a favor—except that he's doing it in the middle of the night. He annoys the housemaster with his request until the housemaster gets fed up and gives it to him. What the man actually gets is never made clear.

So I guess I got my chance. I set a date with my dad to give him a blessing, then proceeded to worry myself sick about it. When the day came, I fasted, hoping to have God's spirit with me. Because, when you give a blessing, there's no telling what's going to happen. Sometimes nothing happens. But someone doesn't ask for a blessing without thinking something is going to happen. So the blesser is in a double bind: on the one hand, he's not sure God is going to will anything to really happen. On the other hand, the blessee is really counting on the blesser to bring those blessings down. I retract—the blesser is actually in a triple bind, because he doesn't know if it's right to invoke healing upon the person. It seems a little presumptuous to tell a person he or she is going to be healed without the go-ahead from God.

The problem is, you don't know what God has in mind until the oil has been applied, the hands are on the head, and the blessing is being spoken. Everything hangs on the spur of the moment: are you ready to receive whatever intelligence it is that God is willing to send down? Sheesh. Talk about a burden. I found out later that Joseph Smith had some of his apostles do a healing blessing over and over again until they finally got the Spirit. But that's just not done these days. It's kind of like baptism: you want to get it right the first time, because after that, it gets plain embarrassing.

Besides that, it was my dad. And I happened to like my dad. I knew that he had suffered from back and head pain for his whole adult life. I really wanted to be part of a process that might heal him.

Finally, the actual minute came. We were gathered in my dad's bedroom; he was sitting on his rocking chair. Another priesthood holder had anointed my dad with consecrated olive oil, and now my hands were on my father's head. I felt my position distinctly. My father had often given me blessings of healing. And every year on the Sunday before a new school year started, he would give each of his children a father's blessing to help them get started (though my math grades never improved). Now I was the one giving the blessing. I cleared my mind, and allowed myself a bit of time to listen. By listen, I mean to God. I was a piece of beeswax waiting for any sort of impression to come. And I was desperate enough to take anything.

Turned out, my dad wasn't slated for immediate miraculous healing. Or even postponed medically assisted healing. Or anything. In fact, I told him this pain was a test, and he needed to suffer through it. You'll find stuff along the way, I said, that will help alleviate the pain, but for now, God loves you. Keep a stiff upper lip. And all that.

Which reminds me, there's another gremlin hanging on the back of the blesser's mind. Namely, what if I don't have enough faith? Maybe I went into this whole deal not believing enough. Maybe I am the cause of the defusing of this blessing. Maybe a mustard seed could leave me in the dust. And, of course, this worry seemed the most probable explanation to me as the blessing ended. Perhaps my faith had failed.

So far I was batting nothing. I decided to just keep this whole incident in my pocket as I went off on my mission to Toronto and be really careful about who I agreed to bless. I hadn't lost faith in the power of the priesthood, but you could say that I became a kind of deist. I started thinking of blessings as moral support rather than a transaction from God, because the few people I blessed always felt the quiet goodness of the Spirit afterward, but the effects didn't last long. I figured this was all right. We'd stick with what we had. But the old stories still knocked around in the back of my mind: those missionaries who actually called the power of God down from heaven.

One day I received a letter from my mom. She told me something weird, that my first blessing was actually seeing some action. Dad had figured out that eating mint or sage brings on a headache. "Remember," she wrote, "that you told him he would find ways to alleviate his pain; well, here it is." I was surprised. Maybe there was something to this blessing thing after all. Then a few months later my mom wrote again to tell me that Dad was installing a Jacuzzi, which apparently does wonders for an achy back. It sounded a little on the worldly side to my poverty-ridden missionary sensibilities, but God is reputed to work in mysterious ways.

About eighteen months into my mission to Toronto, my companion and I were dawdling away a muggy summer afternoon knocking on doors inside a large apartment complex. It was tedious going; hardly anyone was at home. In fact, at one door a housecleaner answered and gave us a royal chewing out for awakening the apartment's occupant, a woman dying of cancer. She slammed the door, and we walked down the hall, feeling like scum but seeing nothing else except to stump ahead. What else were we going to do, preach on a street corner in heat so wet your shirt stuck to your skin? No, we preferred this air-conditioned somnambulism. It was not a little annoying to hear the door open behind us again. No doubt the housekeeper was going to inform us that she had called the manager and we were to be expelled at any moment.

"Hey, come back," she said.

We looked back. Her face seemed different. She told us to come in and pointed at the woman lying in a rented hospital bed. She was a short, round Guyanese woman in her sixties. Her dark skin contrasted with the white floral-print gown she was wearing.

"Elders," she said, "elders, Jesus brought you. Thank you, Jesus."

Apparently Jesus had brought us to that apartment. But now what were we supposed to do? The first thought that comes to any missionary's mind when he is in a situation like this is, I wonder if this person wants to be baptized? It's not a subtle thought, but missionary work is not a subtle job. The problem was, I had no idea what this woman was trying to say. She had a thick accent and couldn't get too many words out at a time. I was thinking about just teaching her the first missionary lesson when my companion finally got what she was saying.

"She's a Mormon." He picked up a book from the shelf, and sure enough, it was that distinctive navy-blue cover with gold lettering. Admittedly, my heart fell a little. We hadn't baptized someone in a while, and I was hoping this encounter was the answer to our prayers. We found out that her name was Evelyn and that she had been baptized a few years ago but had moved, contracted cancer, and lost contact with the church.

Over the next few weeks we became regular visitors and started to meet Evelyn's family. There was her husband Raja, her son Rohan, and Gita, his wife. Rohan and Raja had also been baptized into the church, but Gita, being a new member of the family, was Hindu, which turned our missionary meters right back on. But for some reason, we never really got around to having lessons with Gita. Whenever we visited, we talked with Evelyn. The only thing she wanted to do was pray with us and tell us about Jesus—and we thought we were the missionaries. It was a strange, exhilarating experience to sit next to her lump of a body, sizzling with cancer, and listen to her praise Jesus. It was all we could do to agree with her as quickly as she praised.

The months wore on, and November arrived. The humidity now cut through clothes and iced everyone who was silly enough to be outside, meaning, of course, the missionaries. Evelyn's health followed the decline in weather. More often she would be asleep when we came over, and she would wake only briefly from time to time. No one complained, though; sleep is certainly preferable to pain. One day we stopped in for no particular reason. The odor of deterioration hit us as we walked in. We found Gita, a stick-thin girl with large black eyes and lips perpetually formed into a kiss, trying to comfort Evelyn, who was groaning and lolling her head from side to side. Her fingers were crushing Gita's tiny hands.

"She hasn't slept for days," Gita told us.

Evelyn saw us and gurgled, "Elders, come pray over me." What she meant was, "Give me a blessing." This time the stakes were way up. My dad's pain had been almost theoretical to me. It was something he could take care of, a sort of test case for me. But now I saw Evelyn sunken so far that she was barely coherent. There's a certain feel to the area around someone in complete pain. It smells, oddly, like the flesh of a child. The pained skin gives off an almost electrical charge. Your own nerves vibrate sympathetically with the pain. We put our hands on Evelyn's head. Since my companion was a new missionary, he wanted me to give the blessing—coward. But I did it. And I said, "The pain will lift. You will sleep. God is watching over you."

Her hands loosened their grip, and her eyes closed. She fell asleep saying, "Thank you, Jesus." I swear this is true.

We weren't always so helpful. A week later we stopped by Evelyn's house to sing some Christmas carols—my companion, Elder Christopherson, happened to be an opera singer, fullback, and retired illegal firework smuggler. When we had finished, one of the more long-winded members of our quartet said a closing prayer, and during it, Evelyn lost her breath. She gasped and coughed with a vigor that meant she needed a hospital. But our prayer giver didn't seem to notice and droned on while Evelyn's family rushed to her rescue and called the fire department. The medics carried her out on a stretcher, and we were left to wonder if our rendition had really been that bad.

The mission office transferred me out of that part of town a few days later. A week after that, I got a call from Elder Christopherson: Evelyn had passed away. But not, he told me, before he gave her a blessing. She'd been in a coma for a week. But when he blessed her, she came out of it, grabbed Elder Christopherson by the shirt, and said, "Fat man, baptize my family." Then she talked lucidly with her family for a few moments, closed her eyes, and died.

I'd really like to end the story there. It's a good, happy ending. Boy gets priesthood, boy struggles with priesthood, boy succeeds. The problem is, life goes on. Things change.

Most of the people I baptized on my mission have fallen away from the church. Even Evelyn's family. They all either wandered off or rejected the church outright. I'm still not sure what to think of that. I had been part of the great story: healing, blessing, converting; exercising the priesthood of God. I had made covenants, and I had helped other people do the same thing. And somehow it had all blown away. My priesthood legacy.

There's a popular saying in the church

that a person's mission experience is the high-water mark in his or her spiritual life. You'll never really progress beyond the faith you gain in the mission field. As disheartening as that idea appears, it seemed true to me during the five years after my mission. Mainly because I finally had the time to doubt.

Doubting is a difficult business in Mormonism, especially if you were raised in the church. There's a sense that the whole gospel, from Joseph Smith's first vision to the latest general conference talk, is completely intertwined. That you can't remove one thread from the tapestry, or the whole thing will unravel. I don't know how many times I taught potential converts that if they believed the Book of Mormon was scripture, then Joseph Smith, who brought it forth, must be a prophet. And if Joseph Smith is a prophet then the church he started must be God's true church. And that was only the beginning of this giant game of dominoes.

Not only is the church a unified work, it is also based on the assumption of eternity. Everything you do has an eternal consequence. That's made more than clear in the temple ceremony. The entirety of eternity is spread out, from the creation of the universe to your own personal entrance into God's kingdom. You make covenants there. And since the temple is, after all, God's house, he's there witnessing every one of them.

But there is also an element of chaos. A popular story used in sermons tells about a young priesthood bearer who watched one of his buddies get struck by lightening. He ran to his friend's side, laid his hands on his head, and healed him. What would have happened, the speaker will ask, had that young man not been worthy at that moment?

Don't get caught with your priesthood down.

The doctors found a tumor growing on my mother's brain a few years after I returned from Toronto. It messed with her gyros and deadened her hearing. And, if it didn't get taken out, it would eventually kill her. My mom has always been a big one for blessings. She once told me that when she receives a blessing, she can feel a conduit reaching from inside her, through the blesser, into heaven.

So naturally, when she found out about the tumor, her blessing rate skyrocketed. And it seemed to work because the doctor's blade didn't slip, he filleted the tumor nicely, and she lived to tell the story. I wasn't close by during this period, so my dad gave her most of the blessings. But a few weeks after the operation, she called on Dad and me to give her another blessing. Recuperating from brain surgery needs all the help it can get.

I entered her dim bedroom. She was sitting on the same chair my dad had been sitting on when I went on my maiden priesthood voyage. She asked us to sit down, and then, with a right angle of black stitch marks striding across her head, she asked us to bear our testimonies.

When people have been strapped to a stainless-steel gurney and wheeled to the edge of death, and then wheeled back to life again, they're changed. It doesn't matter if they didn't see a light at the end of the tunnel or angels descending. There's just something about being there, doing that, having the scars to show, that gives this particular kind of traveler a third eye. The kind, I thought as I sat in my parents' room, that can see into your soul. Perhaps it's all the time they've spent in solitude, pain whittling away their bodies so all that's left is spirit. And now, though my mother's eyes were closed, I thought that I could feel this heightened sense turned on me. And that I didn't measure up. I wasn't the person I had been when I was a missionary. I no longer had that singleness of heart, or that purity of faith. It had been alloyed with doubt, disappointment, and questions. Don't get me wrong—I certainly hadn't shaken off any of my Mormonness. When you grow up listening to stories from the Book of Mormon and the Old Testament, they never leave you. The heroes still bang around in their armor, and old bearded men prophesy in Hestonian tenors. But I was different.

I stumbled through a testimony that sounded nothing like the confident assertions of faith we hear every month in testimony meeting. It was full of hopes and wishes, but no beliefs or confessions. All I could call myself was a Mormon by yearning. My dad, on the other hand, said simply, "I know God lives and that, through his son Jesus Christ, I can be saved from my sins." The brevity clinched his surety, and my mother settled into her chair, sustained.

I anointed my mother, placing a drop of consecrated oil on her head and rubbing it into her scalp. But that was all. My father gave the actual blessing, and during it, even though my hands were on my mother's head, I felt like I was watching from outside the circle. I wanted to be inside; but wanting wasn't enough. I couldn't be a pure conduit for my mother. She wouldn't have been able to feel it.

Yeah. The priesthood is a weight.

Sometimes I wish I didn't have this weight. Sometimes I wish I could drop it: the power, the responsibility, the tradition, the expectations. I wish I could cut all the ropes and just fly for a little while, scope out the scenery and choose a nice place to visit. Sometimes I envy the people who can leave the Mormon church, who can forget about their priesthood, who can find a new tradition that suits them better, or create their own. What would happen if I didn't have to wrestle this angel anymore?

∙ ∙ ∙

I admit that one reason I hold onto my priesthood looks a lot like superstition. And it might be. There is a piece of my heart that believes—irrevocably, I think—that this priesthood will one day save either my life or the life of someone I love. And as I've pointed out, perhaps it already has. I can't imagine holding the sick or dying body of one of my children or my wife and not being able to bless them. There's this chance that God will reach down through me, if I have the faith of a mustard seed. Perhaps it is a weakness in character to feel that way. Maybe I'm using my idea of the priesthood as a crutch. As if I'm hanging on to God and my priesthood like an old salad shooter, hoping it will come in handy someday.

But, then again, the priesthood could be a social construction, something that keeps Mormons organized and the men on top. Sort of like how my polygamous ancestors firmly believed that people who didn't enter into plural marriage were unworthy of the highest orders of heaven. I'd like to think that perhaps they were a little wrong about that, as my monogamy is pretty well in place. I want to tell myself that plural marriage was a social construction helpful in keeping the Mormons organized and the men on top. But you don't practice plural marriage unless you believe in it. There has to be some unquestionable core, something transcendent that gives all the pain and wondering some meaning. If I believe in the priesthood only as a social construction, I wonder if it will fail me because I failed it. In which case, why hold on to superstition? It won't work anyway.

This is reality: I doubt. I yearn. My doubt is not going away any time soon. Things I once thought were permanent fade. My stories, which once fit into the larger story, are becoming too complex.

It's anticlimactic to start over, I know. You can't keep the original drama, and you run the chance of boring the audience. But what if I cleared away all the scenery? What if I emptied the whole room and left all the stories behind? Is there any place I can begin again?

Well, sometimes, at night, I watch my two boys as they sleep, and I can't resist the impulse to lay my hands upon their heads, first one, then the other. Though one hand can cover most of the top of a small head, I use both hands. At once I feel completely connected with them—as if I am in the midst of the most intimate gesture that can occur between two people. And it seems, during those moments, that the weight is lifted, or shared, or completely buoyed. No healings. No miracles. No stories.

 I'll start here.

Smoke and Mirrors

First-place winner in the 2006 Eugene England Memorial Personal Essay Competition.

SOMETIMES REVELATION WORKS through a void. Like the day I realized that I knew next to nothing about my little brother.

It's been said that early in my life I held baby Ronnie—number four of nine—in the hospital just a few hours after he was born. But I don't remember the incident. In fact, my memories of Ronnie seem more constructed than recalled, dominated by a composite image my mind probably cobbled together out of pictures from my mother's photo albums and thousands of sandy memories buried in my subconscious. Ronnie had dark-brown hair and eyes to match, like my father's. Brown in the way your grandfather's overcoat was brown. A pliable, supple leather;

warmth. The ancient and the infant. And an oval face with a hint of baby fat. A hint that never left.

But the feature attraction was Ronnie's mouth. We called it a Cheerio mouth. A perpetual O of many interpretations. An O of concentration; reciting the sacred Om; or caught by surprise, open for a sharp intake of breath. Or perhaps an awed whistle. But always, always his mouth was a tender shape. A mussel pried from its shell.

You'd think that being in the middle of the family, Ronnie would have been buffered from life by the caring siblings around him. But he wasn't.

One twilit evening, I followed baby Ronnie up the stairs at the back of the house. All of one year old, he was a semiprofessional walker, still in early training on stair climbing. My mom called out for me to hold Ronnie's hand as he ascended the steps. Whether overly optimistic about Ronnie's skills or preadolescently underenthused in the cooperation department, I decided he could do it himself.

Have you ever looked back on a particular incident and felt you can discern an intricate web of weights and pulleys wheeling away toward a foreordained outcome? It's the type of incident that makes you wonder if guardian angels have evil twins—the distant cousins of angels of destruction—yea, even the angels of stupid, preventable, lifetime-guilt-inducing accidents. Well, this was one of those incidents.

For at just that second, little Ronnie tripped, driving his round lips and baby teeth right into the ignorant corner of a concrete step. Blood, wailing, I-told-you-so's, and a front tooth that zombified into a dull gray during the course of the night.

I stared at the ruthlessly optimistic headlines on the cover of an old *Reader's Digest* holding down a rowdy batch of *Field & Stream*. Beneath the *Digest*'s promises of immortalizing health tips and a daring rescue story lay a picture of a ravenous trout mere milliseconds from clamping its triangular jaws onto a deftly crafted fly, its subtle steel hook glinting inside. Little Ronnie's howls stabbed out of the dentist's office. The poor kid. Only one year old and getting his tooth yanked out. All my fault.

After the sacking of Ronnie's mouth, my

dad carried him into the foyer. The dentist had bestowed a complimentary toothbrush upon my little brother, a reward for courage under pliers, and he had put it to immediate use, scrubbing the toothbrush vaguely in and out of his trampled mouth, staining the new, white bristles.

And that wasn't all Ronnie had to suffer. My sister has the distinction of accidentally helping him chop his pinky off with a slam of a door. He wore a cast for months afterward, and when his finger emerged, it had a question bent forever in its neck.

Through all this, Ronnie remained Ronnie. The quiet kid in the corner, hands in pockets, watching everything with his dark eyes, lips poised.

But as I said, somehow I missed him. Perhaps I was too busy fighting with David, or playing with the baby twins, or sinking into a state of New Wave–induced teenage torpor. Or being just plain gone. Any of these things.

We sit on white chairs in a white room. Giant mirrors on the walls blaze at each other, reflecting our images infinitely until, oddly, they're lost in darkness. Each of us is wearing the sacred temple clothing. White robes; green satin aprons with embroidered fig leaves, reminding us of our mortality. Slippers to keep our feet warm and the white carpet sterile.

My mom and dad are here. My brother David and his wife Veronica. My sister Julie and her fiancé Paco.

We Mormons believe that each person who has lived on the earth needs to be sealed to one another, linking together a long chain of human beings. To be more specific, Malachi said, "He shall turn the heart of the fathers to the children, and the heart of the children to their fathers, lest I come and smite the earth with a curse" (Malachi 4:6). We need the entire human race to be sealed together as one gigantic family in order to find ourselves perfected and brought into heaven. We're either saved together or not at all. A tight spiritual ecosystem, we humans.

One Lord. One faith. One family.

Strangely, this ceremony is something we've never done together before. My parents married in the Salt Lake Temple in 1974.

Since they married under the new and everlasting covenant of marriage, each of the children born to them was born under that covenant. We came into the world already sealed to our family. But it's only now, thirty years later, that we're finally kneeling together, clasping each other's hands, performing the covenant that has been with us so long.

My mother and father kneel at the altar in the middle of the room and clasp hands. The mirrors carry their images as far as reflected light can take them, as if they transcend space. Then, as the sealer speaks the words of the ceremony, they transcend time. They are now, respectively, a man and woman who lived somewhere in Wales, 1869. They each take the hand of their spouse in place of the deceased, in the sight of God and angels, who will validate this marriage for eternity.

After a few ordinances, the sealer stops and tells us that in all likelihood, the people we are doing these sealings for are present in the room. That they are most likely rejoicing at becoming a member of the saved, at having become united with their families.

And in a way, we're each a part of their family now.

We start sealing children to parents. My brother and sister-in-law become children to these two Welsh parents. Each kneels at the altar and places his or her hand on top of my parents' hands to be grafted into the family.

There are lots of names to do that day. We get them from Brazil, Mexico, France, and Germany. And everyone gets a turn at each post. My wife and I are sealed for a couple from Mexico. Then, strangely, my father kneels next to us and places his hand on top of ours. He's sealed to me as my son. This sudden switch of roles catches me off guard.

I remember that bizarre thing Jesus said. "I am the Father and the Son" (Ether 3:14).

In fact, by the time the sealings have ended, we've all been sealed to each other in a variety of ways. A celestial game of genealogical Twister. My sisters and brothers have become my daughters and sons, mothers and fathers. I've sired my own parents. If a string ran between us signifying each relationship we had just contracted, we'd be hopelessly entangled—or tightly bound.

True to the faith that our parents have cherished;
True to the truth for which martyrs have perished.

"I was so proud of you when you went on your mission," says Ron. Yeah. He's Ron now. Twenty-four years old, father of one, divorced of one, proud leader of his own death-metal band. Smoker of cigarettes. Drinker of coffee. In two words: black sheep. All nonjailable acts that stop a person from being a temple-worthy Mormon, Ron has committed.

During that twenty-four-year period in which I had misplaced my brother, Ron had managed to move to Spokane, Washington, under a vaguely gray cloud made up of "inappropriate" music, creative leather neckwear, midnight disappearances, parent-child stresses exacerbated by Ron's idiosyncratic view of financial responsibility, and finally a brush with death. A brush, Ron says, because his thick skull managed to withstand the impact of a swinging chair, as in a western saloon fight. I can still see the earthworm-pink scar like a dripping of wax on his forehead.

"You know, I was running around in a white shirt and tie, too," Ron says, creaming his coffee, a serpent of white coiling into its bitter black. "When I first got up here, I sold stuff door to door. I'd get into this shirt and tie, strap on this huge old duffel bag full of crap, and hit every store on the street."

A piece of the world suddenly falls into place for me. I had always understood the No Soliciting signs on private residences, the ones we missionaries so studiously ignored—"But we're not soliciting; we're not selling anything!"—but not the ones on businesses. They were to discourage people like my brother.

"I'd sell books, toys, candy, all this stuff they could buy and then sell at a huge profit."

"So you'd just go into these stores . . ."

"And I'd dump my crap on the counter and talk and talk and talk." He takes a test sip of the coffee. "Man, I was a hard sell." A glint of bemused pride flashes in his eye.

I try, but I just can't picture Ron as a hard sell.

"It wasn't easy," he says. "It was totally against my personality, but I had to do it. I had to survive."

Over a plate of sausage and eggs advertising the joys of trans fats, he tells me about the time he drove a supervisor to Montana, not realizing that his supervisor was leaving his wife to hook up with another woman.

" 'Course, when I got home, I found out my apartment building burned down. Everything I had was gone. My posters. CDs. Guitar." Ron shrugs his shoulders after the manner of one who has ceased being surprised at the cards life pulls from its sleeves.

In fact, as they couldn't account for Ron for a few days, the police wondered if he had been killed in the fire.

"What did you do?"

Ron shrugs and bites off a piece of glistening sausage. "I lived on the streets."

This has been a night of revelations. My brother was (1) a hard sell, (2) presumed dead, and (3) homeless. I look at him a little harder. Though I've been staying with him for the past four days, I haven't really looked at him. I've kept my childhood image of him in front of his face all this time.

I start to piece together his new face. A wispy Zen-master goatee flows from the chin, eyes the same grandfather brown, but face leaner. Lips, curling next to each other as if for warmth, still occupy only a tiny space above the chin.

Why is it so hard to look? Perhaps because in the curve of the jaw, the squint of the eye, the hold of the shoulder are sown pieces of you, bearing fruit you had never conceived of. There are a million filaments connecting you two, and when either of you changes, there's a pull.

The whole world is being dragged out from under me. Right here in Shari's Diner. Maybe I'll need more than just this strawberry milkshake.

The garage where Deaconess Fatality sets up for the show is different from their home garage only in that the door can open. Our entertainers for the night consist of a lean, muscled drummer; a lead guitarist who, after a few head-banging tunes, resembles

Cousin It; a rhythm guitarist steeped in a more classic-rock era (read: the eighties); a screamer—they were once called vocalists—decked out in eyeliner; and of course, Ron on bass guitar. About a dozen people show up, most of them Ron's night-stocker friends from Wal-Mart.

Transformation gives birth in small places. Socrates in the streets, Jesus in the stable, Joseph Smith in the grove of trees, the Sex Pistols at St. Martin's College.

As they begin their machinations, the members of the band, previously a stubbly clutch of misfits, slowly merge, flexing into one organism. Bound by the veins of their equipment, soon the nine thousand pistons of the beat snap between them, muscle sweat sanctifying the air. We inhale.

There's a reason Deaconess Fatality turns down the lights for a concert. They generate their own.

And as I answer the darkness of the unknown,
I will answer without fear.
I can feel my soul is changing,
I can feel my soul is changing.

• • •

Until now, the beating of my heart has been a tepid thing. The contours of my breath, candy and flaccid. My soul fat upon Fred Meyer. But behold: the voice of him that crieth in the wilderness; a vision rages in the desert; a double-pedaled bass drum rips the heavens asunder!

The cup overflows, and the twelve who stand nearby, yea, even Wal-Mart associates, car-wash attendants, and burger flippers, receive of a fullness: nothing withheld. Sealed in body, spirit, and acceleration, we dance on the threshold of revelation.

The night is clear and quiet. Not a car engine breaks the silence. Not a cricket chirps. Well, I guess I can hear a bit of ringing, somewhere far away in the background. Yeah, there's definitely a ringing.

The band members are dismantling their equipment after inflicting epic sonic damage onto an unsuspecting Spokane suburb. Not being of the death-metal crowd, I had not been aware that, lacking a crash helmet, a wad of unused toilet paper in each ear is a proper accessory for these functions—along with a beer in hand, tank top, metal studs, rings, and other hardware variously inserted into different tender morsels of your body, plus a high tolerance for unintelligible lyrics.

Ron stands in the garage of my transfiguration, smoking and talking with a friend. He tilts his head back and forms his lips into an O. I can see his entire life in that gesture. Then he does something I can't quite catch, and from his lips wings a languid circle of smoke. It flows from his mouth like liquid, like a white serpent, like the slow whip of the northern lights. I've never seen anything so beautiful in my life.

"You can blow smoke rings?"

He smiles and shrugs.

I set up a work light to point toward the ceiling and mount my video camera on a tripod.

"Blow them into the light," I say. Ron thinks it's funny, but he humors me.

I watch the smoke's fetal ballet, its blind, prophetic paths, as it conjures its way through the viewfinder.

• • •

Julie's decision to get married is quite a revolution. Her most intimate contact with boys until now has been to bat them away with a behemoth backpack. This guy Paco must be made of strong stuff. But also, this is the first time almost the entire family has been together in a year.

We've kind of dispersed, as modern families seem to. Thus we've spent countless hours during the past few days racing in the hotel pool, stumping each other with questions from Battle of the Sexes, and generally acting like little kids. Even Ron is here. He took three days off work and drove twelve hours with his girlfriend in a rented car to make the event. No small sacrifice on his part.

Our grandparents are here too. The ones from my dad's side. And this is important. It's important because Grandma has been working nonstop for the past six months to get herself worthy to go to the temple.

"I've just spent too many weddings waiting outside the temple," she says. She wants to be a part of the family. She wants to see that marriage ordinance again. The one that bound her to her husband more than fifty years ago. The one that promises to keep her family together in heaven forever. The one Julie and Paco are just about to enter. This is a time for all of us to be together. To bind ourselves to God, and thus to each other.

There have been five weddings in our family. Ron's was the first one out of the temple. It was one of those affairs with protocol plastered everywhere. Brief, blunt, social rituals. Giddy words flying hard and fast—that is, when the air isn't altogether dead. You know, the way a realtor works on a fixer-upper for one weekend to improve its curb appeal.

Ron's future parents-in-law lived in a house surrounded by a pasture that had been flooded by a nearby river. The day before the wedding, for the heck of it, Ron and I grabbed a canoe and paddled out into the middle of the pasture.

It was one of those moments that should mark the turning point in a Hallmark holiday special. I, the straight-arrow brother, with a mission, temple marriage, and legitimate child under my belt, was supposed to reach out and help Ron see the world through a different pair of glasses. Give him the motivation to turn around and make something better of his life.

But somehow I misplaced the script. My missionary instincts failed me. Turns out we were just two guys sitting out in the middle of an impromptu pond.

The Hallmark camera crew packed up and went home.

For lack of a better plan, we decided to paddle to the river that had overrun its banks. A fine time to discover that Ron had never technically been in a canoe before. I was still knocking the rust off my Boy Scout skills trying to remember how to steer the darn thing when, sensing two suckers, the current caught us.

It was fun at first, zipping along the river. I felt a certain sense of freedom and adventure. But our lack of experience caught up with a disturbing lack of finesse. We crashed through some overhanging bushes and saw that we were heading straight for a culvert. Maybe high enough to let the canoe through. Maybe. And doubtless spattered with slugs, snails, spiders, and other icky sticky things.

It was worrying.

Ron made a grab for a bush. I paddled frantically for the shore.

Finally getting my chance to be a wise big brother, I cried, "We might have to jump!"

"My new boots!" Ron cried back.

The culvert sucked us closer and closer to its dark mouth.

Two idiots in the same boat.

Julie and Paco walk toward the temple door. Hands clasped. The Portland temple is white, an arc light to the world, projecting God upon the sky. Being weird, the couple has forgone the tie and dress. Instead, they have donned long white shirts that look vaguely Muslim over their slacks. To me, they look like modern Nazarites, children of covenant. They're travelers now. Home will soon be in each other.

I can't quite bring myself to go in with them. Ron and his girlfriend are sitting out in his car sharing a cigarette. I toy with the idea of staying out with him. But I wonder how it would look.

From my family's point of view, it would be suspicious, perhaps even an act of betrayal. To come all this way to participate in a once-in-a-lifetime event and then duck out at the last minute. You don't dis God, his ordinances, the salvation of the human race, or your sister (with or without her backpack).

I don't know how it would look from Ron's point of view. A needless sacrifice? A brotherly gesture?

From God's point of view?

I don't know. I don't know at all.

I stand at Ron's car window, making small talk. Feeling like an idiot. I'm supposed to be in the temple. I dressed for it; I prepared for it. My family is in there.

Most of it.

Ron exhales a stream of white smoke from circled lips. It curls like a fern into the air. A breeze catches it and carries it toward me. It hits my white shirt and settles, sealing itself among the fibers.

"You'll be here when I come out?" I ask.

"If you don't take too long." Ron shrugs. Then he turns and grins at me.

So I walk into the temple. I feel its weight, its buoyancy. An elderly man dressed in a white suit looks at my recommend and sends me through. Straight into the house of God.

A filament of tobacco smoke trails from my body, connecting me to my brother.

On the Virtues of Easy Listening

A LOT OF IDEAS AND EMOTIONS go through people's heads when their grandmothers die. Some ruminate over fond memories. Others regret the loss of an extraordinary cook. All plan preemptive strikes on the inheritance.

I plead guilty to each of these charges. After all, Grandma Swenson's "Day-Old Macaroni and Cheese, Lima Beans, Chili and Tuna Goulash, Fortified with a Dash of Wheat Bran" simply had no peer. And the legends of the "Bottle of Cayenne Pepper Stew" along with "The Night of the Living Peanut Butter Meat Loaf" are still told at family reunions. I hope Grandma's eternal reward includes a cookbook and a few lessons with Julia Childs. But the day my grandmother died, what really got to me was that I was two thousand miles away and therefore unable to get a jump on the files.

I had personally helped build those files: clipping by clipping, article by article, pamphlet by pamphlet, until my grandmother and I had succeeded in creating a megalithic bastion of information to rival the Library of Alexandria.

A quick tour through my grandmother's house reveals the magnitude of our undertaking. In the television room we find three full-sized filing cabinets; in the dining room, six. The master bedroom sports another five, and the spare bedroom two. That's sixteen cabinets that come immediately to view. We are not counting the other nests of information breeding throughout the house: the three issues of the Provo, Utah *Daily Herald* that lie on the folding table next to the recliner, the bulging accordion files of articles awaiting transport, the *Reader's Digest*s stacked next to the toilet, or the countless desks, tables, and bookshelves that tremble under the weight of still more fodder for the omnivorous brain of my grandmother.

• • •

I was about fourteen when I first started into my grandmother's service. If you had looked up the word *gangly* in Webster's Dictionary that year, you would have found my name listed along with "see also: geek, acne, body odor." I didn't have much going for me at the time. But for some reason, I could exist without offending too many gods inside my grandmother's house. Perhaps it was because the house was as confused as I was. It was a stubborn brick tank of a place with a cement front porch; the windows were old and wavy, giving the world outside a myopic, slightly seasick look. The décor inside suggested that the blind lived here: a motley crew of steel and wooden desks, stalagmitish floor lamps, desperately seventies sofas, and just about anything else the Salvation Army would be happy to slap a ninety-percent-off sticker on.

And then there was the music my grandma listened to, which could probably put even Barry Manilow into cardiac arrest. I was convinced at that time that intelligent people listened only to sophisticated orchestral music, not the flute and xylophone-riddled pabulum of FM 100. Such was my aesthetic discomfort that one day I asked my grandma why she didn't heave herself a rung higher on the musical food chain. She replied, "I don't do classical—it's too disorganized."

Grandma in a nutshell.

So, with "The Light Touch" as her muse, my grandmother went about practicing her own brand of slash-and-burn reading. When a piece of newsprint caught Grandma's eye, her pen leapt up, almost of its own accord, and scribbled a subject above the headline of the article. The phrase would be something like: *Politics—Utah, Books to read, Hygiene—oral.* Then wielding a pair of scissors with the finesse of a first-grade teacher, Grandma would carve out the article and send it fluttering into her in-box.

This was where I came in. It was my job to alphabetize the articles in the accordion file and then start the delicate process of cramming each article into its appropriate folder somewhere inside the sheet-metal bowels of the filing cabinets. Grandma actually paid me to do this, and she was Scottish. She loved her files that much. The problem was, between Grandma's reading habits and my filing methods, we were lucky to get anywhere.

Sitting atop a stool with corrugations that bit through my jeans into my rump, I read almost as much as she did. Starting in the A section, I was able to file with little regret the articles with subjects like aneurysms, atlases, and Abraham Lincoln, but then the word *acne* would catch my eye. Of the many genetic inheritances I received, a chronic case of pimples was one of the most prominent at the time. I was inhabited by what my sarcastic dermatologist called "a smattering." It was as if Grandma was thinking of me when she saw that article. Who else among her progeny could have taken such an interest in it? In any case, I read it.

In fact, I read probably one in every seven articles—especially when I got to the B and S cabinets, where the "body" files and . . . others were located. They always had some pictures and descriptions of interest to a hormone with legs, though all clipped only from health magazines. Of course, I was very cautious about my reading habits. Whenever Grandma came through the room, I became a busy little bee, flitting from file to file. But when she disappeared, I somehow got stopped on files I had never seen before: true crime, strippers, letter to the Pope.

My heart was not so hard that I did not start to feel a little guilty for stealing this time and money from my grandmother. Every now and then I would try to make up for my wrongdoings by filing as quickly as I could, passing over many an arresting article in the process (conspiracies, nuclear holocaust, Tammy Faye Baker—a swimsuit model, I hoped). But inevitably the siren of information drew me in, and I fell back into my evil ways.

One day, Grandma caught me. I didn't even hear her coming. But, suddenly, there she was, standing in the doorway just watching me. I looked up, guilt stricken, wondering if I was about to lose my cushy job.

"Whatcha reading?" she asked. I showed it to her: an article on suicide. She glanced it over. We talked for the next half-hour about suicide, something every healthy teenager thinks about. Then she handed the article back. "That was fun," she said.

At that moment it dawned on me that I hadn't been hired only as a way for pieces of paper to get around; I had been enrolled in Grandma's University. Student body: one.

After that, I was a faster filer. No longer dogged by remorse, I found that I picked out interesting articles more discriminately (dating, movie stars, mortuaries) and filed the dull ones quickly. Lunchtime with Grandma was a pleasure—in spite of the meal. I always had a million ideas to talk with her about from that day's reading, and she was always willing to chew on them . . . and the fish heads.

However, the files weren't only for me. Though she loved her labyrinth of information, if someone mentioned an interest in a subject that Grandma had covered in her cabinets, he or she was sure to get an appropriate manila folder the next time he or she saw her. Grandma always said she wanted them back, but as curator of her collection, I know that returns were rare.

But that never bothered me. The files for bunions, Buddhism, and beer may have disappeared. I might have to eat a few more meals featuring generous helpings of fifteen-year-old texturized vegetable protein. I might even have to stand by helplessly while a meat grinder of flutes, xylophones, and trombones processed Jimi Hendrix. But if it meant I could spend another afternoon with my grandma, it was all worth it.

Last Supper

"Have you heard the really bad news?" Doc asks as he winds the film in his camera.
Then comes that pause.
"Wayne and Elaine Fairbanks were killed in a head-on last night." It's as if he's talking about what we were going to put in the weather section.
Doc used to sit at the computer next to Wayne Fairbanks's, comparing notes and puns, putting out a newspaper each day.
"He came to see us just a few days ago." Doc kneels to take a picture of a little boy wandering under the boughs of a huge blue spruce. The Christmas lights make the scene cheerful, though the cold has not yet come in to make the lights look warm.
"Eighteen-year-old boy. New truck. Probably drinking. They were on the way home

from Arizona with their two boys. He swerved into their lane. And walked away."

We're reporters. We munch on details like jellybeans. But this time, we leave them be.

The next day I hear Doc on the telephone with the Paige, Arizona, police department trying to extract some information from an unhelpful dispatcher. "The Fairbanks fatalities," he has to repeat over and over.

The picture we publish in the paper was cut from overexposed family photographs, Wayne's benign smile stretching like a jack-o-lantern's across his round, bald head, Elaine's small red lips outlining short teeth, her eyes asquint. It reminds me of the picture we took at the Golden Corral a few months earlier. We had just finished a farewell lunch, commemorating Wayne's move to another (better-paying) job. We all stood in the shrubs, trying to squeeze inside the viewfinder. Smiling, having everything humans could want: hair, fat, bad photograph, a group to smile with.

One of Wayne's sons is on a mission. He hugged his family and got on the plane to Chicago to preach eternal life. He writes letters to them—one probably still on its way through the mail system. I picture him stretched out like a puppet. The strings, once only miles long, snapped; waving in the wind.

I know the feeling. When I was a year into my mission, my grandmother's lungs began to harden. She fell into bathtubs; needed help on the stairs and, finally, help breathing. And then my mission president called me and used his least businesslike voice.

That pause.

"Are you going to be OK?"

"That's what the gospel is all about, sir," I said.

But the strings snapped. Outside, the snow was frozen to the ground; the streets black and slick with ice, reflecting the glow of the streetlamps.

Wayne and Elaine have left a centuries-old station wagon, a house with bread and milk still in the fridge, credit-card offers in the mailbox, and maybe no will.

The family has to ship the bodies—remains—back home to name and prepare, up the same road they were traveling when they were so abruptly wrapped and packaged, as if they had driven suddenly into a dark cardboard box.

It's the family legend that my grandfather was about to take a shower, felt sick, and lay down. A few hours later, my mother wondered who had left the water running, opened the door, and walked three feet from his purpled face to turn the tap off.

"You can get a towel under him and drag him if he's too heavy," said the hospice nurse, almost as old as Grandpa himself. But we carried him. His back, pressed to the bathroom tile, had taken on its coolness. I took the coward's end, the feet and legs, while my uncle Phil took the top.

But what can be touched and handled for the last time on bodies that were killed instantly? Bent and mixed with slabs of metal, pierced and lacerated along with Naugahyde, flung and compressed around the other soft bodies. Stopped. A puzzle the paramedics have to take apart: tearing, slow fluids, unnatural weights, and finally white, reddening sheets.

We found a way to clothe Grandpa, like dressing a sleeping child. Hefting his arms, rolling his head, lifting his torso. Bodies, lying under the weight that breathing had once buoyed, remind the living of what pure flesh is. *This body is shaped like mine, but it does not move. Bodies, my mind insists, move. Bodies move.*

We sat by Grandpa's bedside. I read the last few pages of a book he had been reading that day—out loud, just in case he was wondering how it ended, my own spontaneous version of *The Book of the Dead*. From time to time, I looked up past his cold, white feet into the blackness of the nostrils and mouth.

What happens when only parts of it are shaped like you? When the rest is twisted, severed, broken? What happens when what gave you life, what taught you to repair a bicycle, what debated with you at the dinner table, weighs two hundred pounds? There are no beds for Wayne and Elaine. There are bags.

We often say, as we look upon the corpse of someone we have known, "That's just not him." We say something has fled, leaving a dry husk. All we have of Wayne, Elaine, and their two boys are memories that are far too close. The kind that trick you into making a telephone call, your stomach suddenly clenching as the phone rings and rings.

Because the body is the touchstone for those still breathing. It's a mirror. Our eyes need to rest on the corpse and test each detail. Our own bodies need to sit close and solitary. The hands need to fold near casket wood. The young need to heft the weight of the body and carry it.

The door is closed, but we must press our faces to it and listen.

Winter Light

Third-place winner in the 2005 Eugene England Memorial Personal Essay Competition.

Watchman, what of the night? Watchman, what of the night?
The watchman said: the morning cometh and also the night.
—Isaiah 21:11–12

1939. My aunt May graduated from Utah State University and got on a train to New York. She wanted to be a writer, so really, where else could she go? She stayed near that huge city the rest of her life, returning home only every now and then when she had the money.

1994. Midnight. My plane left Salt Lake International Airport for Atlanta, en route to

Toronto. *Rudy* was the in-flight movie. But since I'd sworn off television and movies for two years, I was staring out the window.

I love to fly, especially at night. Sometimes the dark below stretches out so far that I feel completely alone. But then a trickle of lights floats across the black; a lone EKG reading, growing and expanding until the finger of light multiplies and becomes lost in the burn of civilization.

Kind of like what I was doing, I thought then: a lone figure bringing light to those who live in darkness. Admittedly, I wasn't going to convert cannibals in the jungle, but I didn't have to go so far in order to find people who didn't have the truth. In fact, in all likelihood, the stewardess who had just offered me some forbidden coffee was one of them. I felt a pang of guilt for not offering her a pamphlet or something. The truth. The light. The right track.

That's what it was like being a Mormon. At least, it was to me. There was an almost tangible difference between those who had the truth and those who didn't. Those who had it were on the train. Their tickets were punched, and the train was moving. On their way. Those who didn't were in the waiting room back at the station, coats on their laps. They used the drinking fountain now and then and read paperbacks. Sometimes they did unspeakable things in the bathrooms. But only because they didn't know any better—the very reason why people who got off the train and went back to the waiting room were in such a pickle. After all, they had eaten in the dining car, received their complimentary engineer's hat, and contemplated their glorious destination, but now they were sullying themselves. They could do exactly the same things the unenlightened could do, but they were losing something they could never get back. Their original purity. Maybe that's why the official term for someone who isn't coming to church is "inactive." They've relegated themselves to a room with obsolete magazines, the must of old cigarettes, and dusty tile. What else can one do there but be inactive?

May was a lost sheep. One who had strayed. Poetry was more important than church. She always wrote fond poems about her family after her visits, yet May couldn't communicate with them. They spoke across a chasm. You can see that separation in a picture of May and her parents when her first book was published. May, taller than her parents, stands in the center, her usual deadpan understating the glee any poet must feel at being bound between two boards. Her mother and father stand on either side, with identical expressions. They still wear their coats, a fedora perched on Dad's head, as if they're just about to leave. None of them is touching another. Three pillars. Three cardboard cutouts.

May's brothers and sisters never stopped trying to bring her back—if not to Utah, then to the church. Knowing that May had a scientific turn of mind, my grandfather once sent her *Faith of a Scientist,* by Henry B. Eyring, and *Evidences and Reconciliations,* by John A. Widstoe, hoping that a rational approach to religion would change her direction. Widstoe, she wrote back, was interesting, a mind worth encountering. Eyring was a bore.

• • •

I spent about six months preaching the gospel in Belleville, Ontario. I missed the mountains of Utah Valley; they had always given me a sense of direction, literally. The mountains always ran north and south. A corridor, a demarcated track. In Belleville, Lake Ontario gave me the same sense of direction—the lake was south, a place to look for if I was ever lost.

Belleville had that whiff of the pastoral town that saturates Norman Rockwell paintings, as if *Winesburg, Ohio*, had been moved north to Ontario for historic preservation. I loved the fact that Canada's VIA train could zip through miles of cornfields, that mist covered the ground during autumn evenings, that Church Street, by gum, had churches on it! Really swell ones, too, with high-collar Victorian architecture. And I loved to drive across the bridge arcing over the lagoon to the island of Prince Edward County.

But one of my very favorite places was Bob Cottrell's home. It was a brown-and-red-brick house that sat comfortably on a street lined with two-story maples, leaves almost buzzing with red energy. Bob was about halfway finished remodeling the house. The main floor was complete with a white fireplace, wood-paneled floors, and track lighting. Upstairs was still in progress.

To us, Bob was like his house—almost converted. He had been on the teaching list for about six months when I arrived. He had attended a baptism; he had heard most of the lessons; he even came to church sometimes. We were always saying to ourselves, "This week Bob's going to get wet." I wanted Bob baptized for two reasons. First, I hadn't baptized anyone yet and I wanted to see what it was like. Second, I really liked Bob. He was a theater guy, and having just finished high school, where I had played Polonius, so was I. He was also uncommonly classy. From his perfectly disarranged coffee-table books to his casual yet thoughtful demeanor as he sat in his overstuffed leather chair, to his up-to-the-minute modern-art wall hangings and taste for classical music, Bob had it all. Except one thing—the Spirit.

Thus, my mission: to help Bob feel the Spirit. Because once you feel the Spirit, everything becomes clear. The mountains become visible; the lake appears, the sun rises, the train pulls in. Next stop, the baptismal font.

Actually, helping Bob feel the Spirit wasn't my real job because we knew Bob was already experienced. The first time my missionary companion and I visited him, he had told us that whenever he prayed, he felt a sense of peace. He also enjoyed our company for the same reason. What he was describing was the Spirit working on his soul, no two ways about it. We had pointed that fact out to him, but he just didn't seem to grasp it. It was strange that he hadn't—Bob seemed to be the prime baptism type: he was spiritual and thoughtful, he was generous, and he kept letting us in the door.

But Bob had an unpredictable turn of mind, and it always seemed to keep him as an unknown variable in our spiritual equations. For example, during Bob's early days of investigating the church, the missionaries had challenged him to be baptized. Bob had thought about it for a moment and then taken them out onto his front porch. He showed them his newly planted ivy, just starting to reach its tendrils to the first rung of the latticework. "That plant is a lot like me," he said. "It's just starting to grow. And I'm not sure where it's going yet. In fact, let's make that my spiritual plant. Let's see how it grows."

The missionaries bought a bag of fertilizer that night.

By the time I arrived, the ivy, just taking on its fall hue, was making its way up the lattice, but Bob still wasn't baptized.

Finally, one evening while we were teaching Bob one of the missionary lessons, I entered the zone. I could feel the Spirit rolling through the room like a tidal wave as I testified of the truthfulness of the gospel. I was almost getting a headache from it. While I testified, I watched Bob, sitting with one leg folded beneath him, the other over the arm of his chair, his fingers poised at the side of his face—the thoughtful posture. He was listening: surely he was feeling this. I stopped. "Bob, you feel that? That sense of peace and goodness? It's the Spirit telling you that what I'm saying is true."

Bob thought for a moment and then nodded, mostly to himself.

So I took the next step, the one you take

while the momentum is fresh and strong. "Bob, will you be baptized?"

I went home disappointed. But in the car Elder Mecham said, "I felt the Spirit in there, Elder Carter. There's no way Bob could have missed it."

I had to agree.

Finally I received a transfer out of Belleville. I hadn't seen Bob for a few weeks, but before I left I called him to say goodbye. He invited us over for dinner, which surprised me—all we were ever doing was trying to baptize him.

The dinner was great. Bob had made it himself. He lit candles, turned off most of the lights in the house, and cranked up the Chopin. When we finished eating, Bob went out of the room and came back with a gift for each of us. They were wrapped in tissue paper with oval pieces of paper bearing quotations from a Romantic poet. Mine was from Elizabeth Barrett Browning. It said, "If there were no God, we would have all this beauty and no one to thank for it." I opened my gift. It was a tape recording of Glenn Gould's rendition of the Goldberg Variations.

"He's an odd musician," Bob said, "because he hums along with the music—and not always on key. You can actually hear it in the recording. That's one of the reasons I like him so much."

Crystal was one of those miraculous finds. The kind that come after a hot day of knocking doors—the kind of door you have given up on until, of course, a kid in a diaper comes tearing around the side of the house.

Crystal and her four children lived in an old, two-story saltbox-style house. It was a dark place. Despite the windows, the wood paneling and gray walls drank the light insatiably. The furniture looked as though it were an organic part of the house, sinking into the 1960s wallpaper, melting into the sagging floors. In a small room just off the living room, an inexplicable white man lay in a hospital bed, his beard flaring like the sun, his eyes like awl points. Crystal never introduced us to him. And he never spoke.

I think the old man was a relative of Crystal's, because she had the same sharp

What of the Night?

eyes. The kind you find on a girl you had ignored through school until one day you see past her self-consciously feathered hair and cheap clothes to a soul that startles you.

The road to baptism was a rough one for Crystal. The poor girl had to give up smoking, alcohol, coffee, and tea—part and parcel of the whole Mormon gig. Her husband threw us out of the house once, convinced that we were changing her for the worse: she wouldn't let him smoke in the house anymore and had avoided a certain marital act because, well, it's a cigarette trigger. I couldn't really blame the guy. Then a well-meaning but overbearing cousin threw the whole anti-Mormon spiel at her one afternoon, causing Crystal to break a few bright-red press-on nails as she clenched the counter edge, waiting for the onslaught to end. The principal at the Catholic school her girls attended threatened to kick them out if Crystal became a Mormon. Crystal also owned up to the real reason she'd let us in the door that first day. "You was cute," she said—referring to Elder Mecham.

But it all came, and passed. Crystal somehow managed to get her children to church every Sunday. She had even convinced her husband to come listen to us a time or two. Her blood ran free of nicotine for the first time in years. And then, one brisk autumn Sunday, all her sins were washed away.

Naturally, to remember the moment, we took a picture of the three of us together in front of the font: Crystal dressed in white, twiggy elbows poking through her dress, preparing to be purified. Ticket about to be punched.

A little while before her mother died, May wrote to her about her own life on the east coast, so far away from home. May told her mother how much she admired her. She could do what May could not, raise children, place herself on a strait and narrow path and follow it. "I do not know whether I am making a big circle with my life (I hope it is not a zero!) simply in order to arrive, in the end, where I started."

2001. Salt Lake City. I got on a Boeing 747 with my wife and two children. Non-

What of the Night?

stop 2,600 miles to Anchorage, Alaska, and from there another 362 miles northeast to Fairbanks. As we flew north, the sun hung on the horizon, never quite moving, even though we travelled until midnight. It was almost as if we were following the sun. Tracking it to its home.

As I've found out, light is an important element to factor into the average Alaskan's life. Living in Fairbanks, two hundred miles south of the Arctic Circle, I don't get the full brunt of northern darkness. The folks who live on the north coast go a few weeks completely without the sun and many more with it merely peeking over the horizon, a smoky red eye. Nevertheless, we in Fairbanks can claim our share of sunlight affective disorder sufferers. At the deepest of winter's dark, the sun visits only between 11 a.m. and 2 p.m. It just sort of lolls over the Alaskan range, and as Fairbanks is covered with tall spruce and birch, we're lucky to see the sun at all most days. It refuses us any heat.

However, I feel sorry for anyone who dies without seeing the aurora. LSD has nothing over it. But most of the time the northern lights are no relief from the Alaskan night. Witnessing them is like watching a dress rehearsal for the apocalypse. Great and terrible. Writhing coils of light. The contrails of avenging angels. Especially because the lights are so large, so untouchable, a towering inferno, but speak only in whispers. It would be a relief to hear the voice of the aurora; it would give one's mind something to distract itself with, something that would lessen the abstract impact of the spectacle. The explosion of a firework or the thunderclap following a lightning strike can convulse our bodies with a primal fright. A guttural instinct wakes for an instant to engage the mind in thoughts of escaping bodily harm. But the aurora does not approach with force; it seduces. It flirts with its veils, moving like the helix of the surf or the muscles of a horse, promising a revelation. And you watch as if you were in the presence of gods. But when the veil is removed, all you see is vast, starred emptiness. The joke is on you. The veil was removed not to reveal its source, but to reveal you.

 That's what heaven's like. Revelation in one hand, a knife in the other.

What of the Night?

Getting lost is becoming easy for me. Coming from a valley walled off by mountains 11,000 feet high, I feel as if I am at sea in the midst of the undulations of the Fairbanks land and skyscape. The hills run in no discernible pattern. The Alaskan Range is too far away to steer by. The sky transforms second by second. I can't tell which direction I would walk if one day I decided to go home.

May: one arm akimbo, deadpan, a view of some anonymous bit of New York City behind her. She had just finished her life. I was only fourteen years into mine. The grainy obituary photo seemed appropriate, as did the backdrop. May was famous, sure. But I imagined her in the next life, blinking with confusion at the familiarity of the scene around her. It was just as her family had always believed. And she, without a ticket.

Toward the end of my service in Toronto, I met a missionary who had just come out of Belleville. Excited, I asked him if he had known Crystal. He thought for a moment and said, "Oh yeah, the crazy lady who ran out on her family."

As I look back now at the picture of Crystal's baptism, study her dark eyes, she looks as if she's standing in front of a firing squad, or perhaps the edge of a cliff. Her hands clamped behind her back, head cocked to one side. Squinting as if into a hard wind.

2003. Sunday. A visit to Utah. The chapel is full; the loudspeakers in the lobby aren't working. It's testimony meeting. People from the congregation go to the pulpit and tell the gathered saints what they know to be true. Sometimes they relate miracles. Sometimes just gratitude. Sometimes they try to sell real estate. But since my wife and I can't hear anything in the lobby, we leave. We don't realize my mom has reserved some pew space for us. She waits the whole meeting.

Mom sits across the table from me, her son from Alaska. "How are you keeping your testimony strong?" she asks. It's such a simple question in Mom's language. I used to be able to answer it easily, such as on the day she and my dad picked me up from my mission and I answered over the space of four hours. Now I need another four, most of it to spend on translation. There are too many words that don't have a single meaning. Too many mountains have been moved. Too many constellations veiled.

Testimony meeting isn't over for that Sunday. Mom has saved hers for me. I can tell that she loves me because she talks for a half-hour straight. I don't doubt anything she says. I know her story. I know her certitude. It's palpable, an actual presence. The old language. The rising of the sun. But she weeps because she thinks she's doing a bad job. "I can't explain things these days. I can't put them in order," she says.

For that tiny moment, I hear her. No translation required. I wish I could talk back.

But she wants me to talk about the sun. The aurora's voice fills me instead.

A year after May's death, her sister Margaret did May's temple work for her. Mormonism has a very merciful side to it. If you don't accept the gospel in this life, you can in the next. So Mormons do baptisms for their dead relatives and often for people they don't even know. They also do the other, higher, ordinances: washings, anointings, and sealings. But there's an addendum to this loophole. If you had been the type of person who would have received the gospel, had you heard it in this life, the ordinances can be valid. Otherwise—you had your chance. And, as I figured it at the time, May had been given a lot of chances. She got off track. She became kind of famous in the waiting room, circling around in there. Falling in love with the vending machine. Ignoring the ticket office. Monochrome, anonymous, concrete.

Back to Alaska, 2,900 miles from Spanish Fork, Utah. My family and I sit in Dad's Jeep, ready to go. Mom comes out to say good-bye. She kisses her grandchildren and daughter-in-law. Then she comes to my door. She hugs me and looks at me for a moment.

"It's enough to make a mother cry."

The Departed

The summer of 2000 I was out chasing some stories for the *Orem Daily Journal* when my editor called.

"There's this play or something premiering this afternoon at the SCERA Theater. Would you go cover it?" he asked.

A play premiering at the SCERA at two o'clock in the afternoon? Weird.

When I got there, I wasn't impressed. I saw three other people milling around the lobby looking kind of lost. Two of them were reporters, who are often lost anyway. That's why they're always asking questions.

Someone opened the doors and ushered us into the theater. When the projector turned on, I realized I wasn't here to see a play. But I was in no way prepared for what I did see.

Now, *God's Army* was Richard Dutcher's

second film, so he was still learning plenty about his craft at the time. But none of that mattered to me as I watched this amazing look into a missionary's life. The only thing that mattered was that, for the first time in my life, I saw the potential of Mormon stories. I saw that it was possible to create a morally complex world using the Mormon worldview as a foundation, to make fascinating characters that didn't convert at the drop of a testimony. I saw that faithful Mormon characters could actually propel a story, something I had never supposed. In other words, I saw a real storyteller at work.

By the end of the movie, I was converted. Mormonism wasn't just Sunday anymore. It was a seedbed for compelling, fully realized stories. It was a place where an artistic renaissance could find root. And I, a humble news reporter, wanted more than anything to be a part of it.

I had the chance to sit down and interview Richard after the movie, but I'm afraid I wasn't very professional. I was too overcome by what I had just experienced. But the question kept nagging at me: What was it about Richard's work that made it so much more powerful than anything I had seen before in Mormon art? As a Utah County–raised Mormon boy, I had seen pretty much everything the church had to offer filmwise. *Mr. Krueger's Christmas* bored me; *Legacy* was big; *On the Way Home* was definitely entertaining and had that guy from *CHiPs* in it. But none of them had given me the vision *God's Army* had.

A few months after *God's Army* had come into theaters, I attended some speeches Richard and his wife Gwen gave at Utah Valley State College (which later became Utah Valley University). One person asked Richard if it had been difficult to get the approval of church authorities to make *God's Army*.

"What kind of approval did I need?" Richard asked. "That was my story. You don't need church approval to tell your own story."

Suddenly it clicked. That was what made Richard's work so different from every other story I had seen come out of the Mormon community. It was his own.

• • •

At first, such a realization may look silly, but as I thought back on my own attempts at writing, I began to understand that I was hog-tied by the storytelling expectations of my culture and my church. I didn't have the ability to write my own story.

In his book *Witches Abroad*, author Terry Pratchett portrays stories as etching grooves "deep enough for people to follow in the same way that water follows certain paths down a mountainside. And every time fresh actors tread the path of the story, the groove runs deeper. [. . .] A million unknowing actors have moved, unknowing, through the pathways of story. [. . .] Stories don't care who takes part in them. All that matters is that the story gets told, that the story repeats. Or, if you prefer to think of it like this: stories are a parasitical life form, warping lives in the service only of the story itself."[1]

I was an actor, moving, unknowing, through the Mormon story. A story influenced by thousands of general conference speeches and church magazine articles, and millions of subsidiary sacrament meeting talks and Sunday School lessons. In other words, a very deeply carved story. Practically a canyon.

So, when I tried to write, the boundaries of the Mormon story made themselves felt mightily, like walls of stone. It seemed that there were only two things to be done: follow that same path, making it a little deeper, or climb the wall. But as we all know, climbing the wall means getting out of the story. But where does that lead? According to the Mormon story, it means falling into the anti-Mormon story. Deep into its suffocating waters and violent currents.

It was either one or the other.

But with Richard's initial push, I slowly began to conceive of the idea that there could be a third way to go. What if I could give myself enough authority to start my own story? I mean really delve into my life, really probe my thoughts, really lay out what my experience seemed to present to me instead of letting the Mormon story take over the interpretation? What if I became a branch of the story, as small and uninfluential as I might be, rather than running with the mainstream?

This is what I spent five years doing as

I earned my M.F.A. and Ph.D. in writing—I realized early on that I had no natural facility for storytelling; therefore, I had to go to school to learn it. I was trying to find my way out of the huge story that insisted on telling me. I was also trying to find a way to not slip into the opposite path, the anti-Mormon story, since they are merely two sides of the same coin—both interested in me only as fodder for their own consumption.

So what happened after all this effort? What great reward came my way? Well, at the moment, I am an essayist of very small renown. I write stuff for *Sunstone* and *Dialogue* sometimes and get paid with contributor's copies—strangely, there is absolutely no black market for these. From time to time, I win an award that, though few have ever heard of it, at least bolsters my bank account for a day or two. Only a very small handful of people even know that I write.

I guess I don't have a lot to show as far as accomplishment and popular acclaim are concerned. The only thing I have to say for myself is that I have bled over each of the essays I have published. I personally wrestled each of them away from the two huge stories that wanted to take them over. They're *my* stories.

It was a lot of work to get these essays out, but that didn't bother me. I loved feeling like I was part of the new Mormon artistic renaissance I had come to believe in during *God's Army*. I only wished I had more to contribute to it. Mainly because for so many years, I have found little that nourishes me in the official church. I wanted the church to be brought back to me through the art that arose from it. And I had hope, because things were progressing. I started to see a nook for myself; I started finding a community.

In a recent essay, Molly Bennion writes about a community of Mormon women she found when she joined the church in 1967: "For about twenty years, I felt part of a community of seekers and finders. We who needed to know, who loved to learn, and who found new questions at the end of each new answer were not alone. It was a heady time."[2]

My heady period, when I felt as if I were not alone, lasted seven years: from the day I first saw *God's Army* to the day I read that Richard, for reasons that I'm sure are complex, had decided to graze in other spiritual pastures.

When I first read about it, I immediately wrote to the Association for Mormon Letters e-mail list defending Richard's decision. But I started to notice a significant alteration in my mood afterward. I felt like I was coming apart. I realized that I was grieving and that the grief was attached to Richard's decision. Now I can echo Molly as she writes, "The headiness is gone. Today church is the loneliest place I regularly go."

See, I'd be fine if Jared and Jerusha Hess decided they were done with Mormonism. I'd be fine if Ryan Little or Kieth Merrill decided to leave. It didn't bug me when Neil LaBute and Brian Evenson left. Why? Because their work doesn't enliven Mormon arts except indirectly. The Hesses' *Napoleon Dynamite* and *Nacho Libre* have pretty much zero Mormon references in them, much less ideology. The religious soldier in Little's *Saints and Soldiers* could have been of any faith. Merrill's artistic connection with Mormonism is strictly through institutional film. And I've watched people try to tease out Mormon ideology in LaBute's and Evenson's work, but I've never been convinced by these arguments; when they write about Mormonism, it's generally as horror.

The bottom line is, none of these people did what Richard Dutcher did. He took Mormonism seriously in all its peculiarity, in all its promise, in all its paradox. He approached it unabashed. He was willing to stick his neck out and make real cinema for Mormons.

During the period between *Brigham City* and *States of Grace*, Richard was on the Association for Mormon Letters e-mail list for a few months. During that time, he told us about a production of the musical *Chicago* he had seen in New York and how amazed he was at the dedication of the dancers, throwing their entire bodies into the dance every second, seeming to end the play on the brink of collapse.

You haven't seen me work like that yet, he wrote, but soon you will.

Then we got *States of Grace*. When I saw

it, I could see exactly what he meant. Every bit of talent and energy Richard possessed was pushed to its breaking point. It was my first *God's Army* experience all over again.

But what was the larger picture? Essentially, *States of Grace* was a box-office misfire. When I went to see it, there were two other people in the theater with me. What happened? The greatest accomplishment in Mormon cinema to date comes into our hands, and we ignore it? There is no doubt that *States of Grace* is gritty. My own brother couldn't handle it, so I can't claim that people who didn't like it are stupid. Maybe *States of Grace* just isn't the way most Mormons like their gospel served up. I can appreciate that. I personally dislike the way the institutional church serves its cinematic gospel. So I guess we can all have our opinions.

But there is no doubt about one thing. Richard had put out a deeply personal story. He had bled it out the way one must in order to make a story true. But then he found himself playing to an empty house. In fact, if you were reading the blogs at the time *States of Grace* came out, you would have found a lot of Mormons attacking Richard for his story. What's worse, apathy or antagonism? Richard got both.

Molly Bennion's essay, from which I quoted earlier, focuses on the disappearance of intellectual women from the church. One of the main reasons she gives for this disappearance is that, as a general rule, the church doesn't value the contributions intellectual women can make. "Inside the walls of our chapels and classrooms, most of the talents we have developed and yearn to share with our brothers and sisters seem not to be wanted."

What do you do when a huge part of your community can't or won't hear the unique voice you've cultivated? What do you do when parts of your community condemn you for exercising your talents? What do you do when your community ignores or reviles the stories that nourish you?

During the 2006 Salt Lake Sunstone Symposium, a session was held in which several people gave their own interpretations of *States of Grace*.[3] I listened to this session later as an MP3, and the responses struck me as being too nice. It felt somewhat like a "Praise be to Dutcher" session. I was hoping for a little more rigor, a little more questioning. But then, at the end of the session, Richard got up and talked about the homeless preacher in the movie who says, "The only thing harder than being without a home is being without a church."

"I just realized that for the past few months, I've felt like I've been without a church," Richard said. Turns out this session was just what Richard had needed. It was the resonance he had hoped for. He had found a "church" among the motley crew who attend the Sunstone symposium each year. People with ears to hear and eyes to see the beauty of his contribution. People who could hear the voice of his small stream of story over the roar of the mainstream Mormon story and find an unexpected, but wholly beautiful, harmony.

"Give, said the little stream." That's what so many of us try to do. But we have strange talents whose currency seems to have little value in the economy of Mormonism. So what do we do with our talents? Do we bury them? That would essentially be burying ourselves. I understand that we have started our own little streams; it's our own fault that we're harder to hear than the mainstream. But though we've departed from the primary current, our source is still in Mormonism.

According to psychiatrist Carl Rogers, the most valuable gift we can give each other is understanding.[4] This is why the story of the atonement has so much resonance. The idea that someone has walked with us through our lives and understood us to the core is a stabilizing and empowering one.

In M. Scott Peck's definition of community, you can't get away from the fact that everyone has to stop trying to convert one another in order to become a true community. A community is a place where people hear each other.[5]

Parker J. Palmer defines a community as a space that should honor the "little" stories of those involved as well as the "big" stories of the disciplines and tradition.[6]

Jesus said, "Judge not, that ye be not

judged" (Matthew 7:1). Perhaps he meant that while we're in the act of judging, we're not in the act of understanding.

All of us want to have a community where we are heard, where we can hear other people, where our individual stories can cross-fertilize, making something new and beautiful. There are a lot of us, and we're very different from each other. That's why there are so many different communities. So many different ways to make new stories.

What I hope is that Richard is moving into a community that can hear him. I hope that he can nourish his community as it nourishes him. In fact, I hope this is the path of all who have left Mormonism.

The very definite possibility that Richard will never make another Mormon-themed film breaks my heart, as does the idea that Mormonism can't serve as a community to the person who helped me learn to tell my own story. Equally sad is that the field of Mormon arts has been left to hard-working but only semi-talented artists like me.

Maybe one of Mormonism's roles in the world, besides producing FBI agents, is to export artists to the world the way the

Soviet Union used to, fostering talent like the composer Dmitri Shostakovich and the dancer Rudolph Nureyev so they could defect to the West and carry on their art without the government constantly looking over their shoulder. Just because Russia had a hard time keeping its artists didn't stop it from producing them.

But still, didn't the continent get a little colder, and its nights a little darker, every time one of these artists left?

Bennion's lament for the departing of talented, intelligent women, and mine for Richard, makes me wonder if, as a church, we need to follow Alma's advice a little more: to "mourn with those that mourn; . . . and comfort those that stand in need of comfort" (Mosiah 18:9). To me, that sounds like a good way to say, "Let's start listening to each other's stories."

NOTES

1. Terry Pratchett, *Witches Abroad* (New York: Corgi, 2005).
2. Molly McLellan Bennion, "A Lament." *Dialogue: A Journal of Mormon Thought.* 39.2 (Summer 2006): 115–22.

3. "Discussion of Richard Dutcher's *States of Grace*," 2006 Salt Lake Sunstone Symposium, 10 August 2006, www.sunstonemagazine.com.
4. Carl R. Rogers, *On Becoming a Person: A Therapist's View of Psychotherapy* (New York: Mariner Books, 1995).
5. M. Scott Peck, *The Different Drum: Community Making and Peace* (New York: Touchstone, 1998).
6. Parker J. Palmer, *To Know as We Are Known, Education as a Spiritual Journey* (San Francisco: HarperSanFrancisco, 1993).

Isaiah, Chapter Six

Then flew one of the seraphim unto me, having a live coal in his hand, which he had taken with the tongs from off the altar: and he laid it upon my mouth.
—Isaiah 6:6–7

Elder Conrad was the only missionary in Toronto with a cellular phone. This was when cellular phones resembled railroad ties. Despite its size, the cell phone was a stealth device unrivaled in the field of missionary work. While standing on the porch of the person who had made an appointment with you and was now hiding in the back room, you dialed their number.

"Hi, Bob? How you doing? This is Elder Conrad. Hmm? Oh . . . On your front porch."

It worked like a charm.

Elder Conrad was the only missionary in Toronto who could tell me in all frankness and benevolence that I smelled like a drugstore. It was fatherly advice coming from a man who packed a Dillon's fragrance counter from apartment to apartment. Expensive Italian suits sought him out of their own accord, falling all over each other for the chance to complement his mink eyebrows and transform his belly into a protuberance of power.

Tonight, a touch of grease glistening faintly on his Oscar Wilde lips, Elder Conrad sifted, one pinky aloof from the fray, through the bones of chickens that had blissfully fallen apart in the curry sauce. A predator at tea.

I was a young pup. Only two months in the mission field, eating for the first time with people who came from a Caribbean island I understood to be located in the same ocean Bob Marley came from. They were a small family, newly baptized. Thus the feast. A celebration of life a newly begun.

My taste buds, having been raised on ground wheat and powdered milk from my family's food storage, were intoxicated by this avalanche of exotic spices. I soon found that I had to express my feelings on this unprecedented experience.

"This is good," I declared. "This is *so* good."

Faced with this eloquent assessment, Elder Conrad switched his own taste buds to scan mode. Files from hundreds of restaurants across Calgary, Vancouver, and Toronto compared and contrasted thousands of aromas, tantalizations, and parsley sprigs with this humble meal upon which the neophyte had pronounced his giddy judgment. The results arrived with the wipe of a napkin.

"It *is* good," said Elder Conrad.

The cosmos took note.

"In fact," he continued, "I have never tasted anything quite like it." Elder Conrad's eyes examined the table, trolling for the rogue element, the seductress that had crept into the cuisine.

"Excuse me," he inquired of our hosts, "what kind of peppers did you use?"

Mina fluttered to the fridge and extracted a seething little pod of capsaicin oil, the kind that comes with nature's own warning label: fire-hydrant red. A habanero pepper.

She set it on the table, and Elder Conrad eyed it, chewing to himself.

"When one is tired of London, one is tired of life," Samuel Johnson once observed. Perhaps the same could be said of Toronto. One can ascend the CN Tower only so many times. The Jays cannot play every night. And it cost fifty bucks to go to *The Phantom of the Opera*. Elder Conrad was old. Perhaps twenty-one. He had seen his share. He had known disappointment, grief, and bus-fare hikes. He had traversed the north shore of Lake Ontario, plying the gospel till his eyes had dimmed. And now, finally, something new under the sun.

He gave me a look that could come only from a man playing Russian roulette who has placed the gun's snout to his temple. He reached out and snatched up the pepper. Mina screamed. Rohan lunged for his hand. But it was too late.

As Elder Conrad chewed, the calculation of taste spread again over his face. Then he swallowed. Mina ran for the fridge and grabbed a bag of milk. But Elder Conrad raised a resolute hand. He would have none of it.

His dark eyes grew deep and contemplative. "I can feel it going down," he uttered, nirvana knocking upon his door.

Suddenly his head flipped back like the lid of a Zippo lighter. His lungs and mouth acted in unison to produce a fairly good imitation of an active steam pipe. It was then I realized that Bugs Bunny cartoons are exercises in verisimilitude right down to the ballooning eyeballs, steam-pipe hyperventilation, and fire-engine face. Yes, I also saw heat waves, 300,000 Scoville units worth.

Elder Conrad lurched for the milk and guzzled it down, the fire in his stomach burning as the children of Israel's nighttime pillar. Mina brought popsicles, which he ate whole, though they evaporated halfway down his esophagus. Ice cubes were mere eyedroppers in comparison to the conflagration in Elder Conrad's bowels.

Any hope of doing missionary work that night seemed to evaporate. Elder Conrad had been overcome. The ember had proved too much for him.

His fashion sense, however, was exceeded only by his faith. Besides, Elder Conrad was my district leader. He was with me that day to make sure I was doing my job. It was his duty to give out good advice and see that I was on the strait and narrow. So after half an hour of gasping like a landed fish, he started us on a project even more tortuous than bolting peppers: knocking doors.

It was an exercise that proved to be completely ineffective. Really, this shouldn't have been a surprise. We almost never got through doors anyway, unless we stumbled upon a recent immigrant who couldn't speak English and thought we were from the Ministry of Welfare. But luck came in the form of a puzzled Sri Lankan.

"What is this you say? The spirit?"

"The spirit," I replied, "is a burning in your bosom."

"Bosom?"

"Chest, your chest!" I said loud enough to hopefully penetrate the Tamil barrier.

The man shifted in his chair.

"It burns?" he queried.

"Well, it's a warm feeling. *Warm* feeling. I felt that warmth as we've been talking about these truths tonight."

"*Amen!*" Elder Conrad struck his chest mightily, as if trying to dislodge something.

As we walked home, Elder Conrad waxed metaphorical.

"It's like being poisoned," he said. "My knees are weak, and feel this"—he grabbed my hand and slapped it to his cheek, slick with perspiration.

"Go ahead, ask me where it is," he said.

"Where is it?"

He pointed. Perhaps a quarter of the way through the intestinal track. And miles to go before it slept.

That night Elder Conrad motioned me over to his bed. "If I die tonight," he said, looking like he was about to, "make sure Elder Gadberry doesn't take my suits."

The next morning Elder Conrad left to rejoin his own companion. He had overseen my attempts at mission work. He had given me some good advice, such as lose the polyester ties. His work with me was done. Almost.

When I got back to my apartment with my own companion, I became privy to Elder Conrad's final offering. Because it was too large for the plumbing. Winnie the Pooh could not have been stuck tighter in Rabbit's front door. It was apparent that the pepper had completely purged Elder Conrad's gastric system in one fell swoop. His intestines doubtless shone like a newly waxed car, his stomach clean as Disneyland.

I tried a toilet-paper roll. Then a stick. But Elder Conrad's final testimony was firm and unyielding. So I gave in and walked to the nearest variety store to purchase a plunger.

As I mashed the remains of Elder Conrad's relic into the sewer pipes of Toronto, I suddenly realized that it embodied a parable meant for my enlightenment. And after much contemplation, I gained an insight that guided me throughout the rest of my mission. I call it "the habanera principle."

Simply put: If you swallow the pepper, you will become clean. But I cannot vouch for your comfort or safety during the process. I can say with complete confidence, however, that there will be a mess to clean up afterward.

The Calling

First-place winner in the 2007 Eugene England Memorial Personal Essay Contest; winner of the 2007 Association for Mormon Letters Personal Essay Award.

And Stephen, full of faith and power, did many mighty works among the children of men.
—Acts 6:8

BUT FOR MY MOTHER'S INSISTENCE, the above bit of scripture would have been engraved upon my missionary plaque and hung in our ward building's foyer for all passersby to admire. It seemed appropriate to me. My name is Stephen, after all, and I was going on a mission where, if all went well, I too would be doing mighty works.

I had always been impressed with the

apostle Stephen; the man had guts. Which, admittedly, were probably spread all over the ground by the time the mob was done with him. His crime? He told them that the Messiah had come but that he had brought an olive branch with him instead of an army. This declaration earned him a quick end to his mission courtesy of an audience that decided to cast its vote with stones. I sometimes wonder if Stephen was surprised at this turn of events.

In a rare nod to humility, I let something less than memorable accompany my plaque's picture and golden map of the Canada Toronto Mission. Still, I was off to a good start. It all began with a mission call signed by none other than the one and only President Ezra Taft Benson. Well, by a signature machine, as I found out later, but that wasn't important. What mattered was that I had been called on my mission by God.

And when God calls, he ain't just whistling Dixie.

In the Missionary Training Center, they divided us into districts of about a dozen missionaries. We lived in the same neck of the dorms, went to the same classroom, ate together, prayed together, exercised together, and even showered together. I was lucky; there were only three other guys in my dorm room, and we had a nice view of the gym. Unlike the room next door, which was filled to capacity with a bunch of weirdoes. The oddest of whom was Elder Corley.

Elder Corley was a head shorter than I was. His buzz cut set off his Opie Griffith ears, making him look about fourteen years old, though his youth was offset by a stony look he had probably perfected in boot camp. He had taken a two-year leave from the Army to go on a mission, but he had brought the whole Army culture right along with him. Thus, in addition to studying his scriptures, fasting, and praying, he also locked his legs around the top bunk to do aerial sit-ups, spit-shined his shoes three times a day, and pressed his shirts every morning. Being nineteen years old, several of us delighted in accidentally scuffing his celestial oxfords and saving ourselves from falling by grabbing onto his stern clip-on ties. But despite our best efforts to get him to loosen up, he would just give us a

Gollum look and mutter something polysyllabic beneath his breath.

Everyone else was pretty normal—if you consider being a missionary normal. Which we did. I mean, we did normal things like light our farts, get into towel fights, and weep like maniacs over Jesus movies. We also had our disagreements—once over the perils of R-rated movies, once over the evils of caffeinated drinks, and many times over whose mission would produce the most converts.

The last one was a real sticky point with us. Elder Corley, Sister Rafferty, and I were the three going to Toronto, which had the distinction of being in a foreign country. But that kind of made us the outsiders, as the rest of the district was on its way to California. So the question was, would the people of Toronto provide us with enough "humble seekers" to compete with the Latin American folks in California, who were famous for being the most "open to the Spirit"?

Our aspirations were summed up by a picture someone had cut out of a church magazine and tacked to the wall. At any given time, you could find a group of missionaries staring at it with their tongues hanging out. No, it wasn't Pamela Anderson in a wet shirt; it was a missionary in a wet shirt. He was standing in the middle of an African jungle pond baptizing someone while another fifty grateful souls waited their turn.

Lo, the gates of paradise.

As the plane circled downtown Toronto, I watched the looming concrete apartment buildings go by, thinking that the city's high-density housing was probably designed on the premise that in 1994, a nineteen-year-old kid from Spanish Fork, Utah, could perform his mighty works more efficiently.

After we landed, the mission president and his assistants took us into a meeting room in the president's home and laid out the glorious plan by which Toronto would be redeemed. I was stunned to learn that here, north of the border—in the land of the Mounties, hockey, and the flag with a maple leaf on it—we were going to baptize weekly.

Take that, you Californians!

Elder Glover laid out the plan in the indisputable language of statistics:

- Talk with three hundred people each week, and
- Twenty will listen to a first lesson, of whom
- Five will listen to the second, leading to
- Four who will commit to baptism
- Three of whom will drop out by the end of the six-lesson cycle, leaving us with
- One baptism each week!

And Stephen, full of faith and power!

This was truly the Lord's work. Let's see, two years at a clip of one baptism each week equals . . . 104 baptisms! I was filled with a sense of humility. No doubt I would be tested, but I was up to the task. "If you are obedient," my mission president declared in his resonant voice, "I promise you will baptize weekly."

Obedience turned out to be more difficult than I had anticipated. I had envisioned mere work: hours of knocking on doors and giving lessons and praying and studying. All that was perfectly doable. But something seemed to be amiss.

Some of my shortcomings were obvious. I wasn't very good at talking to people on the street. They all had stuff to do, places to go, and subways to get them there. Often I could muster up the courage to talk only with people who had the new-immigrant stare.

I didn't think my sins were that bad, since I always did my best. But obviously I was wrong because a whole month went by and not one person hit the water, leaving me with four baptisms to catch up on.

One day as my companion and I were leaving the apartment, he offered our usual prayer: "God, please lead us to someone today ready to be baptized."

Suddenly angry, I turned on him. "Look, what's going on? Every day we pray for someone to baptize, and every day we come home empty. Why doesn't God lead us to someone?"

My companion, a seasoned missionary, answered me with his usual reserve, "Elder, God leads us to three hundred people who are ready to be baptized each week. They just don't accept."

You might call that a turning point in

my mission. It was the first moment I wondered, in the small of my heart, what faith and power were up to and when the mighty works would start showing up. You know, the promises.

Not to say that things were bad after that. I worked as hard as could be expected, and I enjoyed parts of my mission very much. I met some people who have profoundly affected my life. I even baptized one or two people who were really worth baptizing.

But I did not baptize weekly.

All right, all right. I can hear it banging around in your head trying to get out, so let's get it over with.

I baptized weakly.

Still—and perhaps it was a reward for my longsuffering with a string of trunky companions one month from home, or, more likely, an act of sheer administrative desperation—I was eventually called to be a district leader, meaning that I was in charge of one other companionship. Well, at least if I didn't get weekly baptisms, I could ask other people why they didn't get theirs either. Besides, the mission office sent this really nice letter to my family telling them about my new calling. They probably hung it up by my shrine in the dining room.

But then, three months before the end of my mission, I got a transfer call. It was a bit of a surprise, as it was so late in my game and especially because I found out that I would be shacking up with the spit-shiner himself, yea, even the king of aerial sit-ups, Elder Corley.

When I arrived at the apartment nestled in a cobwebbed basement, Elder Corley sat writing in his journal at a kitchen table that hailed from the outer reaches of a 1960's sitcom. He labored over his words with methodical single-mindedness. There was no boy left in those ears. The steel of his glasses formed impenetrable rectangles.

I claimed the easy chair for Spain.

And there we sat.

As time passed, I realized that nothing was beckoning us out the door except a sense of duty as gray as the winter sky outside. So, seeing as how I was the district leader around here, I did the only thing I knew how to do: I walked out the door. Elder

Corley set down his pen, closed his journal, picked up his backpack, and followed me.

That evening, I found out that our area was chock full of townhouses and that townhouses are full of people with jobs. People from third-world countries living in planet-sized apartment buildings who think you're from the Ministry of Welfare—now there's fertile ground. But people with jobs—well, they have a retirement plan and therefore see no need for a salvation plan.

An hour into the evening, the unspoken became unbearable. I looked down the block, door after door after door, and I knew none of them would open. I didn't even bother looking behind me, because back there was another endless row of doors, all closed.

Elder Corley and Elder Carter. Suits frayed, shoes holed, eyes dimmed. Angels round about us, priesthood burning in our bones, golden God-callings hanging in foyers back home. Put out to pasture. Shoved into a corner. Flyspecks in the Book of Life. I had an inkling of what I'd find if I looked in Elder Corley's journal.

Of all the conversations we might have over the next few months, I knew that we would never talk about the MTC. About the promises. About that poster with all the converts lined up to receive their golden ticket to the celestial kingdom. Sure, we had baptized some people. We'd had some good experiences. But what about the promises? The strangled promises, the corpses of our weeks. Baptismless. Dragging along by chains around our ankles.

His name was Elder Stewart. At three months, he was a district leader. At six, our brand-new zone leader. And we knew he'd be an assistant to the president in no time. All he had to do was prove himself just once more. Flooding our zone with the waters of baptism.

"We're going to baptize like crazy in this zone," Elder Stewart proclaimed. "Because we're going to do what no other zone has done." Dramatic pause. "Each companionship is going to teach at least one hundred first discussions each week!"

The crowd gasped. A few of the young missionaries jumped forward on their chairs, their shiny new ties catching the sun.

"I've been praying hard about this, and if we teach a hundred first discussions each week and testify like crazy, I know we'll get at least twenty second-discussion appointments. Heck, teach them both discussions on the bus, who cares! Then at least five will commit to baptism; of those, four will . . ."

Elder Corley and I looked around to see if we had somehow wandered into a *Twilight Zone* episode. But we could feel the electricity filling the room. That old black magic. The heady stuff that had jackhammered through our veins at the MTC. And we could see it sizzling in the other members of the zone, too. The streets of Toronto were no longer safe.

On the bus, I sat across the aisle from Elder Corley. The stone that had held his face was thinning, the boy reaching up. His heart was pumping like mine. I knew what we were both thinking. We wanted it all back. Every minute of our missions. We wanted the promises.

And Stephen, full of faith and power?

When we got home, we sat down and made a covenant with each other. We swore that we would keep every rule. We'd get up right on time. We'd use every minute of the day exactly the way it was laid out for us in the missionary handbook. We'd say our prayers. We'd walk our shoes until they crumbled. We'd talk to everyone we met. We'd fill ourselves with faith. We'd really believe the promises. We'd expect them to come to pass. Just as God said. Just as our mission president had promised.

We wrote out our plan and sent it in to the mission president. "Please," we wrote, "just let us stay together so we can carry this plan out and reap the blessings. We only have two months left."

Transfer night came and went with no call from the mission office, and Elder Corley and I found ourselves in the position of actually having to carry out our plan.

And we did, deviating not one iota. An army of two. Plus God. You should have seen us.

Fast forward one perfect month. The phone rings.

"Elder Carter? This is Elder Caldwell. How are you? Great!"

Something was afoot. Why else would an assistant to the president call a mere district leader? My stomach did its impression of a bowl of Jell-O with carrot shreds as I waited to hear what was on Elder Caldwell's mind.

"We think you've really done a great job as a district leader," he said. "And we know that the Lord is pleased with your service."

Well, there you go. You apply a little elbow grease, and look what happens. True, we hadn't baptized yet that month. But there were still two days left. And we had done our part.

"We think it's time for you to move on now, Elder Carter. We're releasing you from your calling as district leader."

I stared at the scriptures in my lap. The scriptures I had been reading so dutifully from exactly 9:50 to 10:05 P.M. for the last month. Elder Corley sat at his table, pen hovering over his journal, which he had stopped writing in as much so he could read his scriptures at the right time.

I closed my scriptures.

Elder Corley set his pen down.

"Sometimes I think," he said, "that I should just take the food from the fridge and dump it straight into the toilet. It would save me a step . . . eat and crap, eat and crap."

You've heard of people who reject their callings—Esau, Jonah, Balaam—but have you ever heard of a calling that rejects you?

Well, take a look. We had done everything right. Obedience and faith were not the question. But, if we thought we had nothing before, now we had less. No numbers, no baptism prospects, not even a measly district leadership to lean on. The belly of the whale was looking good right about now.

In the quiet of our subterranean apartment, Elder Corley and I decided that the system could go perform an anatomical impossibility upon itself. Whichever one it chose. We were finished with the whole affair. We didn't care that our zone had a meeting every week to rejoice in its rising statistics. We didn't care that we had to report to our chipper new district leader every night. We didn't care about that lousy piece of imperialist propaganda stuck to the wall at the MTC.

And Stephen, full of . . .

We went out the next day and visited Peter. Peter, the guy with the glass eye. Peter, the guy whose prize possession was a gold-inlaid special edition of the three-level chess game featured in *Star Trek: The Next Generation.* Peter, who had a stack of business cards proclaiming a computer-consulting business that he was going to get off the ground sometime tomorrow. As soon as he potty-trained his dog. We just sat and talked with him. We listened as he harangued the televised parliament session with hard-hitting commentary. We brought a tuna sandwich from Subway to share with him. And he cooked us something he called lasagna.

It was a good day.

The next day we went to the local hospital and signed up to push a cartload of smutty romance novels and candy bars around the hallways. Our mission: to linger. To listen to half-sedated West Indian women talk about their childhood pets. To discuss the merits of Danielle Steele's clothing descriptions and how Harlequin Romances could kick Silhouette's pantied little hiney any day of the week. To spend fifteen minutes helping a patient go through every drawer and nook in her room to find that last nickel she needed for a Mr. Big candy bar. At times, we found that nickel in our own pockets.

And then there was Janelle, the biggest, nicest lady in the only apartment complex in our area. She always had a project up her sleeve or a computer standing at the gates of death.

And Rene, she had a mom named Martha, hooked up to an oxygen machine, who never got any visitors. Of course she'd enjoy a visit from two nice young men. And her husband Stan needed someone to talk politics with. Politics was an area where we could provide some help, as one of the recent premiers of Canada shared a name with a prophet-warrior from the Book of Mormon. (Well, his name was Mulroney, but we didn't know how it was spelled, so it was close enough for us.) They talked Canada, we talked pre-Aztec Central America, and everyone seemed to understand one another.

Our zone was now legendary throughout the mission for its hundreds of first discussions each week. There was only one blemish on its righteous face: us. All the shiny ties glowered at us—the goats on the left hand of the zone leader, the hisses and bywords.

But just when we thought we'd really hit our "don't give a damn" stride, things started to fall apart. Isn't that always the way it is? You think you've eluded those pesky angels by burrowing deep into the whale's intestines. And then a light appears at the end of the esophagus.

Martha wanted to get baptized. She was pretty sure she was going to meet Jesus pretty soon anyway, and she wanted her eternal passport stamped. Could she make Jesus happy by getting baptized even with her oxygen machine? Then Rene's friend Anita got hot for church, too. It reminded her of AA meetings except without coffee and donuts at the end. And some guy out of the freaking blue just called us up to get his teenage son, Jake, ready for dunking. And Janelle? She had a friend too, April.

Peter, however, had only his dog.

At the end of that month, Elder Corley and I sat in our final zone meeting, old, tired, and finished. Elder Stewart tallied the stats for all the companionships on the blackboard. Under the column with the heading "First Discussions," each companionship broke the hundred barrier with ease. The shiny ties bounced up and down in their seats.

Elder Corley and I had four. The bouncing stopped.

The second-discussion column registered around twenty per companionship. Smiles all around. Elder Corley and I had four. No smiles.

The thirds made the unexpected plunge to the lower end of the single-digit spectrum. Elder Corley and I had four. Fourth discussions were somehow nonexistent—except for the four reported by the two trunk-meisters in the corner. Not to mention the fifth and sixth discussions and the forgotten baptism column. Great big goose eggs until the last companionship.

Four. One baptism a week for a month.

I looked around the room and was surprised to see fury in almost everyone's eyes. "Who are you," their glares raged, "to flout the rules and yet baptize weekly?"

They had a point. If not for this string of baptisms—a fluke at best—our mighty works would have consisted of raising Janelle's computer from the dead, surviving Peter's lasagna, and ministering formula fiction and candy bars unto the sick and afflicted. Our principles, if you could call them that, held no promise of baptism. It was in righteousness that the missionaries of the Canada Toronto Mission desired an army, but Elder Corley and I, like Stephen of old, found ourselves standing in front of them holding an olive branch.

Perhaps the mob had its own wisdom, knowing that an olive branch has never succeeded in running a mission. That to accept the branch would be to accept that no one knows through which vessels faith and power will flow. To accept that when we dip our empty cups, we may receive water, gall, or wine.

That we can never know what we bring to our lips.

And Stephen, finally empty, rejoiced and dipped his cup again.

Writing as Repentance

FOR ME, WRITING IS REPENTANCE—even though I dislike that word. When I hear it, I remember all those priesthood sessions of general conference when I sat between my dad and my brother in the darkened chapel, staring up at the huge faces telecast from Salt Lake City, their resonant voices filling the room. Scared utterly out of my mind.

I was convinced at the time that I was one of the vilest of sinners. I often couldn't sleep at night, so aware of my sins that my stomach churned. I was afraid that if I fell asleep, I would die and find out just what a complete waste of God's energy I was.

I spent many of these sleepless nights composing a will—really more of a confession, because I had very little to bequeath and few siblings worthy of it. I'd scrawl out my sins in a notebook and then stuff it into my orange lockbox, hoping my confession would buy me some leniency at the judgment bar.

But I was pretty sure it wouldn't. In my fitful sleep, I would sometimes dream that I had just died and was standing in downtown heaven. All the people there smiled at me. "Of course you're going to pass the judgment bar," they cooed. "You're such a good boy with nothing to hide."

Then I heard heavy footsteps behind me: the angels sent to escort me. (Remember, Mormon angels don't have wings.) My judgment time had come. I ducked into a nearby mansion and listened to the angels thundering by, giant smiles on their faces, looking for that nice kid who would surely pass judgment and go straight to heaven. But the longer I hid, the grimmer their faces became. It was only a matter of time before they found me.

I had racked up quite a collection of spiritual infractions, you see. Like the peanut-butter sandwich I had made on the sly when I was supposed to be fasting. And the pocket change I had swiped. And the swear words I had learned. And the sins incident to—

perhaps even required for—adolescence. These sins were like invisible strings tying me to the ground. They looked thin enough, but when the time came, would I be able to snap them? Or would I stay fastened to the burning earth while the rest of my family and friends flew into the sky?

Do you remember the old gray woman in Jim Henson's movie *The Labyrinth*? The one who waddles around hunched beneath the weight of a pile of junk? That was my soul—distended and cancerous, hobbled and bent with the accumulation of sin.

Obviously, I had a very platonic concept of spirituality. The metaphors I used for thinking about my spirit presupposed a bright core, a perfect version of myself—the one that had accepted Jesus' plan in the premortal council. Sin was the stuff that distorted, dimmed, and calcified that core. Repentance was like going to Gold's Gym and working off all that flab to reveal the true me beneath; it was the chemotherapy that burned away the malignant cells I had been cultivating inside me; it was the wire brush that raked away the scum. I was always looking for a way back to purity, a way to unburden myself.

∙ ∙ ∙

In my mid-twenties, having not yet died and gone to hell, I decided to go to grad school, as being a news reporter simply wasn't paying the bills. So my wife and I applied to some schools and received offers from universities in Washington and Alaska. Going to Alaska seemed scary at first, especially since we had two very young children. But you only live once, right?

During the months before we moved, I dreamed about Alaska. In one dream, my family and I had just arrived in Fairbanks, and it was beautiful. The golden, horizontal light of sunset bathed the city, and people walked blithely along the streets. But suddenly the light utterly vanished, leaving only darkness, and I fell to my knees trying to feel my way to my family, trying to feel my way home. But I didn't know which way home lay.

That dream followed me as we flew to Alaska. I wrote in my journal of the flight:

We didn't see much because the dark gray clouds smothered everything. I started to think of Alaska as a dark country, map-

less and roadless. Like the blank spots that used to denote the unexplored regions of Africa, or like polar maps.

The undulations of the clouds' surface seemed to be a snapshot taken of boiling sewage: thousands of bloats about to erupt. But then I noticed that the black nodes weren't patterned randomly, but followed each other in wormish curves, as if they were the corrugations of a dark brain brooding over an empty land. At one point, the clouds broke up momentarily, and far below I saw what seemed to be fragments of dim glass and, snaking through them, the insane scrawl of a metallic river.

Very soon after I started my graduate program, I felt pulled toward writing about my experience as a Mormon. Which surprised me, because I moved to Alaska expressly to get away from the overwhelming Mormonness of Utah. But the pull was undeniable. It wouldn't leave me alone.

However, as I wrote, I realized that even though I was the person typing, I wasn't in control of my stories. I could feel them being fought over by two forces. One was the sacrament meeting mentality that wanted to take all my stories, scrub them shiny, and tie a pretty moral around their heads. The other was the deconversion mentality that wanted to dismiss my Mormon experiences as naïve pit stops on the way to true enlightenment. So insistent were these mentalities that I felt the stories were trying to tell me, instead of the other way around.

After a lot of writing and rewriting, I eventually compiled a small collection of personal essays that were as finished as I could get them. I bound them into a chapbook and gave copies to a few friends one Christmas. Upon reading them, one friend who had very cordially left Mormonism a few years before wrote this to me: "The picture I had in my mind as I read these essays was of you standing on the edge of a cliff, kicking rocks off, taking a few running starts, but always stopping short. Never jumping. Why don't you jump?"

The question took me by surprise, and I had to think about it for a long time. Why didn't I jump? Why didn't I just burn down the house and start all over again—whether it was the world's house or the Mormon house? It would be such a relief to just say to one or the other, "I know thee not"—to declare that I could no longer serve two masters and finally, with one house gone, settle in the other.

An artist friend said that while she was reading the essays, a very strong image came to her. She painted it for me: a slight human figure faced by two overwhelming mountains (*see page 166*). Entranced, I immediately hung it up in my living room and began contemplating it. After a few weeks of this, I finally saw what was going on in my writing.

Those mountains were the contradictions in my life. Sometimes the priesthood is a wonderful thing to me. Other times, it's an oppressive weight. Sometimes I can feel the binding power of the temple. Other times, it seems only to cut me off from my loved ones. My mission was at once an elating and awful time.

In order to really finish any of my essays, I had to forego the satisfaction of an answer, promised at the top of either mountain. In-

stead, I had to forge into the canyon, filled though it was with mist and darkness. Because that was the only place not already built. It was the only place I could create myself without the dominance of one mountain or the other.

So, I take my journeys into the canyon, but not alone. I carry my pile of sins along with me.

There is only one way of knowing an essay is finished, and that is when I have wrought something new from the contradictions of my life. When I have dwelt long enough in the shadows of the mountains to see the beauty of both. When I have finally changed enough to collect the used tin foil, the ratty teddy bears, the rusty bicycle frames, the dog-eared magazines, the empty toilet paper rolls of my experience and make something that derives its beauty not from the perfection of its materials but from the interplay of their imperfections.

The answer I finally gave to my post-Mormon friend was, "If I jumped, what would I have to write about?"

When judgment day comes, the angels will have to find me by following the little monuments I've constructed with each act of repentance. They'll have to track me through canyons and alleys, finding my works in dark, tension-filled places. But why should that be a surprise? God started creation with the firmament: undefined, chaotic, and bellicose.

So, when I say that writing is repentance, I mean that repentance is best defined as creation. I mean that the sins I carry on my back are not junk; they are my tools. I mean that the unexplored canyon between those two domineering mountains—dark and frightening though it often is—is the only place I can work out my salvation.

About the Author

Stephen Carter didn't leave Utah until he was seventeen and went to Disneyland. It wasn't much different. His next out-of-Utah experience brought him to Toronto, where he volunteered as an LDS missionary. After a stint as a full-time news reporter, he earned an M.F.A. and Ph.D. from the University of Alaska–Fairbanks, where most of these essays were written.

Carter's work has been cited as notable writing in *The Best American Spiritual Writing 2006* and honored by the Association for Mormon Letters. He has received the Young Writer Award from *Dialogue* and several awards in the Eugene England Memorial Essay Contest. Carter is currently the editor of *Sunstone* magazine.

www.ingramcontent.com/pod-product-compliance
Lightning Source LLC
Chambersburg PA
CBHW051435290426
44109CB00016B/1570